Boudica: The Life and Legacy of the Celtic Queen Who Rebelled Against the Romans in Britain

By Charles River Editors

John Opie's painting of Queen Boudicca

About Charles River Editors

Charles River Editors provides superior editing and original writing services across the digital publishing industry, with the expertise to create digital content for publishers across a vast range of subject matter. In addition to providing original digital content for third party publishers, we also republish civilization's greatest literary works, bringing them to new generations of readers via ebooks.

Sign up here to receive updates about free books as we publish them, and visit Our Kindle Author Page to browse today's free promotions and our most recently published Kindle titles.

Introduction

Boudica

John Winfield's picture of parts of the Roman wall in London

"[The Romans] thinking that it might be some help to the allies [Britons], whom they were forced to abandon, constructed a strong stone wall from sea to sea, in a straight line between the towns that had been there built for fear of the enemy, where Severus also had formerly built a rampart." – Bede's description of Hadrian's Wall in the Middle Ages

The famous conqueror from the European continent came ashore with thousands of men, ready to set up a new kingdom in England. The Britons had resisted the amphibious invasion from the moment his forces landed, but he was able to push forward. In a large winter battle, the Britons' large army attacked the invaders but was eventually routed, and the conqueror was able to set up a new kingdom.

Over 1,100 years before William the Conqueror became the King of England after the Battle of Hastings, Julius Caesar came, saw, and conquered part of "Britannia," setting up a Roman province with a puppet king in 54 BCE. In the new province, the Romans eventually constructed a military outpost overlooking a bridge across the River Thames. The new outpost was named Londinium, and it covered just over two dozen acres.

For most of the past 1,000 years, London has been the most dominant city in the world, ruling over so much land that it was said the Sun never set on the British Empire. With the possible exception of Rome, no city has ever been more important or influential than London in human history. Thus, it was only fitting that it was the Romans who established London as a prominent city.

Londinium was initially little more than a small military outpost near the northern boundary of the Roman province of Britannia, but its access to the River Thames and the North Sea made it a valuable location for a port. During the middle of the 1st century CE, the Romans conducted another invasion of the British Isles, after which Londinium began to grow rapidly. As the Romans stationed legions there to defend against the Britons, Londinium became a thriving international port, allowing trade with Rome and other cities across the empire.

By the 2nd century CE, Londinium was a large Roman city, with tens of thousands of inhabitants using villas, palaces, a forum, temples, and baths. The Roman governor ruled from the city in a basilica that served as the seat of government. What was once a 30 acre outpost now spanned 300 acres and was home to nearly 15,000 people, including Roman soldiers, officials and foreign merchants. The Romans also built heavy defenses for the city, constructing several forts and the massive London Wall, parts of which are still scattered across the city today. Ancient Roman remains continue to dot London's landscape today, reminding everyone that almost a millennium before it became the home of royalty, London was already a center of power.

The Romans were master builders, and much of what they built has stood the test of time. Throughout their vast empire they have left grand structures, from the Forum and Pantheon in Rome to the theatres and hippodromes of North Africa and the triumphal gates in Anatolia and France. Wherever they went, the Romans built imposing structures to show their power and ability, and one of their most impressive constructions was built on the northernmost fringe of the empire. Shortly after the emperor Hadrian came to power in the early 2nd century CE, he decided to seal off Scotland from Roman Britain with an ambitious wall stretching from sea to sea. To accomplish this, the wall had to be built from the mouth of the River Tyne – where Newcastle stands today – 80 Roman miles (76 miles or 122 kilometers) west to Bowness-on-Solway. The sheer scale of the job still impresses people today, and Hadrian's Wall has the advantage of being systematically studied and partially restored.

One of the reasons the wall existed was to protect against enemies, and given what happened in the mid-1st century CE, the Romans' fears was understandable. Indeed, Londinium had become the largest city in Britannia shortly before being burned down in a native revolt led by an infamous Celtic Iceni queen named Boudica.

With a name meaning "Victory," Boudica was a charismatic woman who commanded nearly 100,000 Celts and led them on a campaign to expel the Roman overlords from Britain around the year 61 CE. Often called the "Celtic Queen," she wore a warrior's necklace around her delicate neck and rode upon a sturdy steed. According to the ancient historian Cassius Dio, "In stature, she was very tall, in appearance most terrifying, in the glance of her eye most fierce, and her voice was harsh." It is said she had a piercing glare that could shrink her people's enemies, which in this case were the Roman legionnaires under the vengeful general Suetonius.

Boudica was not only a woman of high intelligence but also a Druid priestess of great repute, which caused the Romans a unique kind of concern. The Celts have fascinated people for centuries, and the biggest fascination of all has been over the Druids, a religious class at the heart of Celtic society that wielded great power. Naturally, people have been interested in Druids for centuries mostly because they don't understand much about the Druids or their practices. The word comes from the Romans, who labeled them "Druidae" in reference to the white robed order of Celtic priests living in Gaul, Britain and Ireland. They were a well-organized, secretive group who kept no written records and performed their rituals - allegedly including human sacrifice - in oaken groves, all of which interested and horrified Roman writers. As Pliny wrote in the 1st century CE, "Barbarous rites were found in Gaul even within my own memory. For it was then that the emperor Tiberius passed a decree through the senate outlawing their Druids and these types of diviners and physicians. But why do I mention this about a practice which has crossed the sea and reached the ends of the earth? For even today Britain performs rites with such ceremony that you would think they were the source for the extravagant Persians. It is amazing how distant people are so similar in such practices. But at least we can be glad that the Romans have wiped out the murderous cult of the Druids, who thought human sacrifice and ritual cannibalism were the greatest kind of piety."

While Boudica fought for freedom, the Romans were willing to fight just as hard for the wealth of the Celtic resources, including troves of gold, silver, and tin. The Romans wanted the various groups of Britain to become Roman vassals, pay taxes, adopt the Roman system of governance, and become like slaves in service of Rome's extravagance.

As a result, the uprising would be bitterly contested, and though the Romans emerged victorious, Boudica remains a towering figure in the minds and hearts of the Celts and the British today. She lived and died, but she achieved historic immortality, and a bronze sculpture sits on the embankment of the Thames River near Westminster Bridge memorializing the queen. The face of Boudica resembles that of Queen Victoria, and she is widely considered a champion of liberty and a symbol of the integrity and perseverance of the British people and of womanhood itself.

Boudica: The Life and Legacy of the Celtic Queen Who Rebelled against the Romans in Britain examines the facts and legends surrounding Boudica and her uprising. Along with pictures depicting important people, places, and events, you will learn about Boudica like never before.

Boudica: The Life and Legacy of the Celtic Queen Who Rebelled against the Romans in Britain

About Charles River Editors

Introduction

    The Origins of the Iceni and Druids

    The Roman Occupation

    Boudica's Background

    Celtic Resistance

    Omens

    Boudica's Revolt

    The Aftermath of the Uprising

    Further Reading

The Origins of the Iceni and Druids

The yellow area represents the Celtic presence in the 6th century BCE, the lighter shades of green represent the expansion of the Celts in the 3rd century BCE, and the dark green represents the Six Celtic Nations and areas where the Celtic languages are still spoken today.

For decades, scholars, linguists and archaeologists have sought to fuse information culled from the surviving Celtic languages, the physical remains of the past, and historic documents to reconstruct the lives and histories of the various Celtic peoples.

The historical search begins by examining language. While people often think of language as constantly changing, with new slang words appearing seemingly by the day, there are many elements of language that are quite conservative and slow to change. These parts include pronunciation, grammar and "basic core vocabulary" (like pronouns, parts of the body and family relations). Basic core vocabulary changes so slowly that linguists can use it to compare and contrast languages and look for ancient links between them. Because changes to these words accumulate not only slowly but also at a relatively regular rate, linguists can compare two branches of a related language tree (like Italian and Spanish) and estimate at what point the two languages diverged from one another. This is a rough estimate, but for particularly ancient divisions, before the invention of writing, it is often the best date available. This process is known as glottochronology.

Almost all European, Iranian and Indian languages descend from a single language called "Proto-Indo-European."[1] For example, linguists have attempted to reconstruct Proto-Indo-European (PIE), and by using some clever comparison and backtracking, they have argued that the concept of the word "around" was originally spoken in PIE as something like *ambi-**[2]. Linguists have found Gaulish examples from modern-day France and Celtoiberian from modern-day Spain that use the term *ambi-* almost identically. In the contemporary Old Irish, which also has written examples, linguists have found the use of *imm-* and the use of am- in Middle Welsh. This pattern also continued into the present day: in modern Scots Gaelic *im-*, in Welsh *am-, em-* or *ym-*, in Breton *am-* or *em-* and in Cornish *am-, ym-, om-* or *em-*. It is apparent that the terms resemble each other, and that their variations have slowly shifted over time.[3]

There are considerable debates amongst linguists as to when and where Proto-Indo-European emerged and began to break into today's language families, with some arguing modern-day Turkey around 8,700 years ago[4] and others the southern Russian Steppes around 6,000 years ago[5].
Regardless, the language communities that would eventually speak Celtic broke from this mother tongue many thousands of years ago and moved westward into what is now Central Europe, where the language emerged into a form that is recognized as distinctly Celtic.

---

[1] European exceptions include Basque, Finnish, Hungarian, Estonian, Saami, Turkish and Gagauz.

[2] Linguists use an asterisk (*) to mark a word that they have reconstructed but have no hard evidence for.

[3] "Examples from the Celtic Core Vocabulary." Accessed online at:
http://www.wales.ac.uk/Resources/Documents/Research/CelticLanguages/ExamplesCelticCoreVocabulary.PDF

[4] "Early date for the birth of Indo-European languages" by Michael Balter for the journal *Science*, (Nov 28, 2003): 1490-1.

[5] *The Horse, the Wheel, and Language: How Bronze-Age Riders from the Eurasian Steppes Shaped the Modern World*, by David W. Anthony (2007). Princeton University Press

A Celtic stele from around the 2nd century CE

Within the language family, recent research indicates that the northern Goidelic Celtic languages (Irish, Scots Gaelic and Manx) broke off from the southern Brythonic languages (Welsh, Cornish and Breton) around 1100 BCE. The Continental Celtic, usually referred to as the extinct language of Gaulish, separated from the Brythonic languages around 1000 BCE. The splintering of these subfamilies into the named languages of today happened relatively recently, with the Brythonic languages separating in the 9th century CE and the Goidelic in the 8th century CE.[6]

---

[6]"On the position of Gaulish within Celtic from the point of view of glottochronology" by Václav Blazek in the

The techniques of historical linguistics, including glottochronology, provide the necessary evidence to link the ancient Celts to various time periods. Because much of modern archaeology works to provide links between archaeological discoveries and particular times, linguistic information allows researchers to go one step further and associate a language with archaeological remains as well. If this sounds complex, that's because it is. This task is riddled with the potential for mistakes, and the archaeology of Celtic remains is often a very controversial subject. As a result, in some cases the word "Celt" has been removed and replaced with more neutral terms like "Iron-Age Peoples", to the consternation of many Celtic nationalists. However, the fact that the Celtic languages exist today means that they have existed throughout history, and with them Celtic peoples. In other words, archaeological studies of the Celts are not impossible but merely difficult, and as techniques have become far more refined in recent years, they have provided an increasingly clear picture of the past.

Due to ancient accounts, there has long been a debate over the location and origins of the first Celts. Roman writers like Julius Caesar used the term Celts to refer to people who the Romans came into contact with in France, while ancient Greek historian Herodotus suggested the Celts were originally near the Rhine River. Today, the first group that archaeologists tentatively connect to the Celts is a cultural group called the Urnfield Culture, which existed primarily in today's eastern and southern France and western Germany. They were known for their cremated burials in urns and were considered to be a Bronze Age people, since they used metal tools constructed of bronze, a mixture of copper and tin, and practiced agriculture. The Bronze Age is typically associated with the classic Dynastic Egypt, the empires of Sumer and Babylonia in today's Iraq, the Pre-Classic Greece of Homer and the Minoan civilization of the island of Crete.

---

journal Indogermanische Forschungen #114 (2009): 257-299; "On Application of Glottochronology for Celtic Languages" by Václav Blazek in the journal *Celto-Slavica: Second International Colloquium of Societas Celto-Slavica*. pp. 11-36. 2006, Moskva.

An urn constructed sometime during the 10th-8th centuries BCE

The Urnfield people existed from around 1300-750 BCE and were expansionist, clearly relying on their impressive hill forts. The division of the main branches of the Celtic languages (set around 1100 BCE) occurred in this period and may be linked to a series of events around 1200-1100 BCE that are known as the Bronze Age Collapse. This mysterious time was a period of massive social upheaval, population movements, and societal collapse throughout the Mediterranean, including the collapse of the Hittite Empire and the Egyptian New Kingdom. The Bronze Age Collapse had repercussions throughout Europe, especially if the cause, as some believe, was due to climate change.[7]

---

[7]"Empires in the Dust" by Karen Wright in the magazine *Discover* March, 1998. "The Influence

Collapses aside, culture change in the archaeological record tends to be a slow process as one "culture" slowly gives way to another. Eventually, the Urnfield people were replaced by a set of cultural remains that archaeologists refer to as the Hallstatt Culture, which thrived from around 900-600 BCE. This was probably not an actual replacement of one group of people by another but an evolution of technology and traditions that saw the old ways remain at the peripheries long after the wealthy areas converted to the new forms. The most noticeable addition was the use of iron tools, which means the Hallstatt are an Iron Age people.

The western branch is typically associated with the Celtic peoples, while the east is associated with another Indo-European group called the Illyrians[8]. In the west, the people used and were even occasionally buried with mighty chariots, and they built hilltop forts like their predecessors. While the easterners began to trade with Greece early, the western (presumably Celtic) Hallstatt people only came into regular contact with the Mediterranean trade routes after 600 BCE.[9] This is important for two reasons. The first is that the control of luxury goods from these areas was apparently a key element in the rise of more centralized government (which are now called "chiefdoms"). Second, it was these Mediterranean peoples who possessed writing and thus began to document the existence of the peoples related to the ancient Celts.

Entering the 5th century BCE, scholars are able to draw more concrete connections between people, place and language based on all three forms of documentation: linguistic analysis of language fragments, archaeology of sites, and the written records of ancient observers, most importantly the Romans. The group that emerged out of the Hallstatt people, known in archaeological circles as the "La Tène" culture, has been directly linked to the Celts of Roman history. This was perhaps the Golden Age of the Celtic peoples, who were at the height of their military power and artistic endeavors and were spread out as far as they ever would.

---

of Climatic Change on the Late Bronze Age Collapse and the Greek Dark Ages" by Brandon L. Drake in the *Journal of Archaeological Science* XXX (2012):1-9

[8]The Illyrians are potentially the linguistic ancestors of today's Albanians. For more information on the theory, see *The Illyrians to the Albanians* by Neritan Ceka (2005), Publishing House Migjeni. Certainly, the Albanians speak a form of Indo-European as distinct from others (and therefore as ancient) as the Celtic family is from the Germanic.

[9]"Hallstatt Culture" in *Cassell's Peoples, Nations and Cultures (2005)*. Retrieved from http://www.credoreference.com.libezproxy2.syr.edu/entry/orionpnc/hallstatt_culture

Reconstruction of a La Tène settlement in Germany

The heartland of their influence was in what is now France and southern Germany, where they were referred to as "Gauls" and their language was called "Gaulish." In Spain, they were known as the Celtiberians, after they arrived during the twilight of the Hallstatt period (the 6th and 7th centuries BCE) and occupied the Ebro Valley the in northeastern area of Spain. The Celtiberians were documented by Roman writers like the geographer Strabo, who noted that they were known to the classical Greeks. It is also believed that Herodotus was referring to the Celtiberians when he talked about the Celts living "beyond the pillars of Hercules" The 4th century BCE Greek poet Ephorus wrote that they had "the same customs as the Greeks." It was likely the Greeks who first labeled people Kelts, and their other references to Iberians likely led to their compounding of the names into Keltiberians, thus ignorantly uniting various distinct nations.[10] The Romans didn't make much of a distinction either, though Strabo did note differences between the peoples in Germany and the Iberian Peninsula, writing, "Now the parts beyond the Rhenus, immediately after the country of the Celti, slope towards the east and are occupied by the Germans, who, though they vary slightly from the Celtic stock in that they are wilder, taller, and have yellower hair, are in all other respects similar, for in build, habits, and modes of life they are such as I have said the Celti are. And I also think that it was for this reason that the Romans assigned to them the name 'Germani,' as though they wished to indicate thereby that they were 'genuine' Galatae, for in the language of the Romans 'germani' means 'genuine.'"

The Celts were drawn further into the Mediterranean world by allying themselves with the Carthaginians in the Punic Wars, which is not altogether surprising since Hannibal and his father

---

[10]This is from Strabo's *Geography* 1:2:27. This translation is from the edition for Bohn's Classical Library, translated by H.C. Hamilton, Esq (1854).

had established Carthaginian power in southern Spain. However, it proved to be a big mistake after Carthage's total defeat at the hands of the Romans; naturally, the Romans had little sympathy for the Celtiberians as they moved to dominate the Iberian Peninsula.[11] Strabo, an important Greek historian and geographer, wrote in his seminal *Geography*, "As for Iberia, the Romans did not stop reducing it by force of arms until they had subdued the whole of it, first, by driving out the Nomantini, and, later on, by destroying Viriathus and Sertorius, and, last of all, the Cantabri, who were subdued by Augustus Caesar. As for Celtica (both the Cisalpine and Transalpine, together with Liguria), the Romans at first brought it over to their side only part by part, from time to time, but later the Deified Caesar, and afterwards Caesar Augustus, acquired it all at once in a general war. But at the present time the Romans are carrying on war against the Germans, setting out from the Celtic regions as the most appropriate base of operations, and have already glorified the fatherland with some triumphs over them."

Despite their divisions, the Celtic leaders were able to mount highly effective military campaigns from their rich heartlands, moving out into Italy and the Balkans in the 4th and 3rd centuries BCE and reaching as far as modern-day Turkey. Celtic soldiers even sacked the city of Rome in 390 BCE. This expansionism was not due to an inherent warlike or emotional nature but to the fact that chiefdom government structures like theirs rewarded conquest as a path for self-promotion. In many ways, their government and social structures were similar to those found around the Mediterranean world in the centuries before the Roman Empire, only that the Celts were particularly effective at utilizing those structures for their own benefit.[12]

Much of what is known about the Continent Celts in this period comes from surviving writings, in particular those of the Romans and Greeks who fought against the Celts throughout that era. Of course, much of the writing takes on the tone of propaganda and is laden with descriptions of drunken, barbaric Celts without the marks of civilization that the Romans and Greeks saw in themselves.[13] Reading about a culture from its enemies is always a tricky business, but after the Roman Empire conquered Gaul (and Iberia) by the 1st century CE, the Gaulish or "Gallic" Celts were integrated en-masse into Roman culture. While the French state classically likes to refer to "Our Ancestors the Gauls" in the 19th century, little remains of their language or culture in contemporary France, even though a shared Celtic past remains a symbolically potent idea.[14]

---

[11]"Celtiberians" in *Cassell's Peoples, Nations and Cultures (2005)*. Retrieved from http://www.credoreference.com.libezproxy2.syr.edu/entry/orionpnc/celtiberians

[12]"La Tène." *Encyclopædia Britannica. Encyclopædia Britannica Online Academic Edition*. Encyclopædia Britannica Inc., 2013. Web. 15 Mar. 2013. <http://www.britannica.com.libezproxy2.syr.edu/EBchecked/topic/326554/La-Tene>.

[13]"The Ancient Celts" In *Cassell's Peoples, Nations and Cultures (2005)*. Retrieved from http://www.credoreference.com.libezproxy2.syr.edu/entry/orionpnc/celts_ancient

[14]"Our Ancestors the Gauls: Archaeology, Ethnic Nationalism and the Manipulation of Celtic Identity in Modern Europe" by Michael Dietler (1994) in the journal *American Anthropologist* 96(3):584-605.

People love reading about the Druids, yet many would have a hard time even defining them, and there is even considerable debate about the etymology of the word "Druid." The first steps of this word are relatively clear: "Druid" in English comes from "Druide" in French (perhaps in the 1560s), and this comes from the Latin "Druidae", which was the term used by the ancient Roman chroniclers. However, the more interesting and useful question is what is the origin of the term in Latin. Did the chroniclers invent the word, or was it borrowed from some Gaulish or other Celtic terminology? If the latter is true, than understanding the origins of "Druidae" may explain how the ancient Celts saw their religious leaders, much the same way insights can be gained from analyzing the Christian title "pastor," which is drawn from the term for someone who cares for a flock of animals and says something about the ways that early Christians viewed their spiritual leaders.

Unfortunately, the modern Celtic languages do not provide much help, because their terms for Druids are typically borrowed from English, as with the Cornish word "drewyth ("drewydhyon" for the plural).[15] However, for over a century, scholars have examined the extant Celtic tongues and compared them to the written fragments of earlier incarnations to attempt to reconstruct a language they call Old Celtic, and by examining the hypothetical words of Old Celtic (for which there are no written records), scholars can propose theories of the origins of words like "Druidae."

One of the most convincing of these arguments is that the word was "Druides" in Gaulish, which was the language of the Celts who fought against the Roman chroniclers, and that it in turn came from a hypothetical Old Celtic word "*derwijes[16]." This would have come from "*dru" (which meant "tree" or "oak") and "*wid-" (which meant "to know" or "to have a vision"). This would mean that the roots would be something akin to "those who know the oak." Interestingly, the Old Celtic word "*derwos" also meant "truth," a double meaning that was probably not lost on the Celts[17].

There is one other potential origin of the term worth noting. The Celtic languages are divided into two large groups: the Brythonic (including today's Welsh, Breton and Cornish and historical Gaulish and British) and Goedelic (including today's Irish, Scot's Gaelic and Manx and the historic languages of Ireland). The term "*derwijes" is derived from the Brythonic side of the language family, which makes sense considering that the Romans primarily encountered speakers of Brythonic languages in Gaul and Britain. However, in the contemporary Irish and Scots languages, the term "draoi" comes from "druadh", which means a "magician" or "sorcerer." This comes from an Old Irish term "drui" with the same meaning. What gives this argument

---

15 In Nance's classic 1952 *A New Cornish Dictionary* (pg 43), the term is further attributed from borrowing from Welsh and Breton.
16 In historical linguistics, words which have been reconstructed in the manner I described, but have no concrete records in the written word are marked with a "*" to denote them as hypothetical.
17 "Druid" in the *Oxford English Online Etymology Dictionary* accessed online at: http://www.etymonline.com/index.php?term=Druid

some plausibility that the first one does not have is that the words "draoi," "druadh" and "drui" can all be found in either modern spoken language or in written records, not merely through hypothetical reconstruction.

Thankfully, there are plenty of ancient sources of information documenting the existence of the Druids, and there is also archaeological evidence. It is from the written record, specifically the writings of Roman chroniclers, that people first learned about the Druids, and ultimately it is from these important but questionable sources that scholars have the only confirmed evidence about the beliefs and practices of the ancient Druids.

Even before the rise of the Roman Empire, ancient historians described the Celts and some of their rituals. According to the ancient Greek historian Athenaeus, in the 4th century BCE, Sopater noted, "Among them is the custom, whenever they are victorious in battle, to sacrifice their prisoners to the gods. So I, like the Celts, have vowed to the divine powers to burn those three false dialecticians as an offering." In the early 3rd century BCE, Timaeus wrote, "Historians point out that the Celts who live on the shore of the Ocean honor the Dioscori above other gods. For there is an ancient tradition among them that these gods came to them from the Ocean."

Another Greek historian noted their use of sacrifices, "Eudoxus says that the Celts do the following (and if anyone thinks his account credible, let him believe it; if not, let him ignore it). When clouds of locusts invade their country and damage the crops, the Celts evoke certain prayers and offer sacrifices which charm birds—and the birds hear these prayers, come in flocks, and destroy the locusts. If however one of them should capture one of these birds, his punishment according to the laws of the country is death. If he is pardoned and released, this throws the birds into a rage, and to revenge the captured bird they do not respond if they are called on again." Strabo noted a similar anecdote: "The following story which Artemidorus has told about the crows is unbelievable. There is a certain harbor on the coast which, according to him, is named 'Two Crows'. In this harbor are seen two crows, with their right wings somewhat white. Men who are in dispute about certain matters come here, put a plank on an elevated place, and then each man separately throws up cakes of barley. The birds fly up and eat some of the cakes, but scatter others. The man whose cakes are scattered wins the dispute. Although this story is implausible, his report about the goddesses Demeter and Core is more credible. He says that there is an island near Britain on which sacrifices are performed like those in Samothrace for Demeter and Core."

Ultimately, the most concrete descriptions of the Druids came from several Roman writers, who offer tantalizing glimpses into the lost religious and ritual world of the Druids and overwhelmingly demonstrate the social power that the Druids had and the ways that Romans seemed to often hold them in awe as well. Perhaps the most detailed discussion of the Druids and their ways comes from Julius Caesar's *Notebooks About the Gallic War*, written some time in the 50s or 40s BCE. He discusses Celtic society and the Druids at length:

"Throughout Gaul there are two classes of persons of definite account and dignity…Of the two classes above mentioned one consists of Druids, the other of knights. The former are concerned with divine worship, the due performance of sacrifices, public and private, and the interpretation of ritual questions: a great number of young men gather about them for the sake of instruction and hold them in great honour.

"A great many young men come to the Druids for instruction, holding them in great respect. Indeed, the Druids are the judges on all controversies public and private. If any crime has been committed, if any murder done, if there are any questions concerning inheritance, or any controversy concerning boundaries, the Druids decide the case and determine punishments. If anyone ignores their decision, that person is banned from all sacrifices—an extremely harsh punishment among the Gauls. Those who are so condemned are considered detestable criminals. Everyone shuns them and will not speak with them, fearing some harm from contact with them, and they receive no justice nor honor for any worthy deed.

"Among all the Druids there is one who is the supreme leader, holding highest authority over the rest. When the chief Druid dies, whoever is the most worthy succeeds him. If there are several of equal standing, a vote of all the Druids follows, though the leadership is sometimes contested even by armed force. At a certain time of the year, all the Druids gather together at a consecrated spot in the territory of the Carnutes, whose land is held to be the center of all Gaul. Everyone gathers therefrom the whole land to present disputes and they obey the judgments and decrees of the Druids. It is said that the Druidic movement began in Britain and was then carried across to Gaul. Even today, those who wish to study their teachings most diligently usually travel to Britain.

"The Druids are exempt from serving in combat and from paying war taxes, unlike all other Gauls. Tempted by such advantages, many young people willingly commit themselves to Druidic studies while others are sent by their parents. It is said that in the schools of the Druids they learn a great number of verses, so many in fact that some students spend twenty years in training. It is not permitted to write down any of these sacred teachings, though other public and private transactions are often recorded in Greek letters. I believe they practice this oral tradition for two reasons: first, so that the common crowd does not gain access to their secrets and second, to improve the faculty of memory. Truly, writing does often weaken one's diligence in learning and reduces the ability to memorize. The cardinal teaching of the Druids is that the soul does not perish, but after death passes from one body to another. Because of this teaching that death is only a transition, they are able to encourage fearlessness in battle. They have a great many other teachings as well which they hand down to the young concerning such things as the motion of the stars, the size of the cosmos and the earth, the order of the natural world, and the power of the immortal gods.

"All of the Gauls are greatly devoted to religion, and because of this those who are afflicted with terrible illnesses or face dangers in battle will conduct human sacrifices, or at least vow to do so. The Druids are the ministers at such occasions. They believe that unless the life of a person is offered for the life of another, the dignity of the immortal gods will be insulted. This is true both in private and public sacrifices. Some build enormous figures which they fill with living persons and then set on fire, everyone perishing in flames. They believe that the execution of thieves and other criminals is the most pleasing to the gods, but, when the supply of guilty persons runs short, they will kill the innocent as well.

"The chief god of the Gauls is Mercury and there are images of him everywhere. He is said to be the inventor of all the arts, the guide for every road and journey, and the most influential god in trade and moneymaking. After him, they worship Apollo, Mars, Jupiter, and Minerva. These gods have the same areas of influence as among most other peoples. Apollo drives away diseases, Minerva is most influential in crafts, Jupiter rules the sky, and Mars is the god of war. Before a great battle, they will often dedicate the spoils to Mars. If they are successful, they will sacrifice all the living things they have captured and other spoils they gather together in one place. Among many tribes, you can see these spoils placed together in a sacred spot. And it is a very rare occasion that anyone would dare to disturb these valuable goods and conceal them in his home. If it does happen, the perpetrator is tortured and punished in the worst ways imaginable.

"The Gauls all say that they are descended from the god of the dark underworld, Dis, and confirm that this is the teaching of the Druids. Because of this they measure time by the passing of nights, not days. Birthdays and the beginnings of months and years all start at night.

"The funerals of the Gauls are magnificent and extravagant. Everything which was dear to the departed is thrown into the fire, including animals. In the recent past, they would also burn faithful slaves and beloved subordinates at the climax of the funeral."[18]

Caesar, while writing something of a puff-piece in *Notebooks*, certainly had firsthand knowledge of the Druids from his time fighting the Gauls and was thus an invaluable direct

---

[18] All of the Caesar quotes are from: *The Gallic War* by Julius Caesar, Book VI Chapters 13-14. Accessed online at: http://penelope.uchicago.edu/Thayer/E/Roman/Texts/Caesar/Gallic_War/6B*.html#13

observer. While probably writing from second-hand sources, Strabo gave a similar description of the Druids' high status in his seminal *Geography*, which was published in the first decade of the 1st century BCE, before Caesar's work: "Among all the Gallic peoples, generally speaking, there are three sets of men who are held in exceptional honour; the Bards, the Vates and the Druids. The Bards are singers and poets; the Vates, diviners and natural philosophers; while the Druids, in addition to natural philosophy, study also moral philosophy."[19]

Caesar's observation that the Druids acted like judges for social disputes was also echoed by Strabo, who wrote, "The Druids are considered the most just of men, and on this account they are entrusted with the decision, not only of the private disputes, but of the public disputes as well; so that, in former times, they even arbitrated cases of war and made the opponents stop when they were about to line up for battle, and the murder cases, in particular, had been turned over to them for decision. Further, when there is a big yield from these cases, there is forthcoming a big yield from the land too, as they think." Strabo also seems to confirm Caesar's description of the Druids' religious beliefs about the immortality of the soul: "However, not only the Druids, but others as well, say that men's souls, and also the universe, are indestructible, although both fire and water will at some time or other prevail over them."

While these theological points may have been of some interest to the Romans, one area of religious practice that always intrigued ancient writers was divination: the ability to tell the future or of far off events. The famous Roman orator and philosopher Cicero described the Druids, amongst the religious practitioners of several foreign peoples, in his work *De Divinatione* ("*Of Divination*"). He wrote in approximately 44 BCE, "Nor is the practice of divination disregarded even among uncivilized tribes, if indeed there are Druids in Gaul — and there are, for I knew one of them myself, Divitiacus, the Aeduan, your guest and eulogist. He claimed to have that knowledge of nature which the Greeks call 'physiologia,' and he used to make predictions, sometimes by means of augury and sometimes by means of conjecture."[20] Strabo also mentioned Druidic divination: "They used to strike a human being, whom they had devoted to death, in the back with a sabre, and then divine from his death-struggle. But they would not sacrifice without the Druids."[21]

Diodorus Sicilus described Druidic rituals surrounding divination at length:

> "The Gauls have certain wise men and experts on the gods called Druids, as well as a highly respected class of seers. Through auguries and animal sacrifice these seers predict the future and no one dares to scoff at them. They have an especially odd and unbelievable method of divination for the most important matters. Having

---

19 All of the Strabo quotes come from *The Geography Book IV, Chapter 4:4* accessed online at: http://penelope.uchicago.edu/Thayer/E/Roman/Texts/Strabo/4D*.html#4.4
20 *De Divinatione* Book I 41:90, accessed online at: http://penelope.uchicago.edu/Thayer/E/Roman/Texts/Cicero/de_Divinatione/1*.html
21 Strabo's *The Geography Book IV*, Chapter 4:5

anointed a human victim, they stab him with a small knife in the area above the diaphragm. When the man has collapsed from the wound, they interpret the future by observing the nature of his fall, the convulsion of his limbs, and especially from the pattern of his spurting blood. In this type of divination, the seers place great trust in an ancient tradition of observation.

"It is a custom among the Gauls to never perform a sacrifice without someone skilled in divine ways present. They say that those who know about the nature of the gods should offer thanks to them and make requests of them, as though these people spoke the same language as the gods. The Gauls, friends and foes alike, obey the rule of the priests and bards not only in time of peace but also during wars. It has often happened that just as two armies approached each other with swords drawn and spears ready, the Druids will step between the two sides and stop the fighting, as if they had cast a spell on wild beasts. Thus even among the wildest barbarians, anger yields to wisdom and the god of war respects the Muses…

"It is in keeping with their wildness and savage nature that they carry out particularly offensive religious practices. They will keep some criminal under guard for five years, then impale him on a pole in honor of their gods—followed by burning him on an enormous pyre along with many other first-fruits. They also use prisoners of war as sacrifices to the gods. Some of the Gauls will even sacrifice animals captured in war, either by slaying them, burning them, or by killing them with some other type of torture."

A better-known account of their divinatory and magical practices comes from *The Natural History*, by Pliny the Elder, who mentions the Druids in his chapter on mistletoe. He noted:

"I can't forget to mention the admiration the Gauls have for mistletoe. The Druids (which is the name of their holy men) hold nothing more sacred than this plant and the tree on which it grows—as if it grew only on oaks. They worship only in oak groves and will perform no sacred rites unless a branch of that tree is present. It seems the Druids even get their name from drus (the Greek word for oak). And indeed they think that anything which grows on an oak tree is sent from above and is a sign that the tree was selected by the god himself. The problem is that in fact mistletoe rarely grows on oak trees. Still they search it out with great diligence and then will cut it only on the sixth day of the moon's cycle, because the moon is then growing in power but is not yet halfway through its course (they use the moon to measure not only months but years and their grand cycle of thirty years). In their language they call mistletoe a name meaning "all-healing". They hold sacrifices and sacred meals under oak trees, first leading forward two white bulls with horns bound for the first time. A priest dressed in white then climbs the tree and cuts the mistletoe with a golden sickle, with the plant dropping onto a white cloak. They then sacrifice the bulls while praying that the god will favorably grant his own gift to those to whom he has given it. They believe a drink made with mistletoe will restore fertility to barren livestock and act as a remedy to all poisons. Such is the devotion to frivolous affairs shown by many peoples.

"Similar to the Sabine herb savin is a plant called selago. It must be picked without an iron instrument by passing the right hand through the opening of the left sleeve, as if you were stealing it. The harvester, having first offered bread and wine, must wear white and have clean, bare feet. It is carried in a new piece of cloth. The Druids of Gaul say that it is should be used to ward off every danger and that the smoke of burning selago is good for eye diseases. The Druids also gather a plant from marshes called samolus, which must be picked with the left hand during a time of fasting. It is good for the diseases of cows, but the one who gathers it must not look back nor place it anywhere except in the watering trough of the animals.

"There is a kind of egg which is very famous in Gaul but ignored by Greek writers. In the summer months, a vast number of snakes will gather themselves together in a ball which is held together by their saliva and a secretion from their bodies. The Druids say they produce this egg-like object called an anguinum which the hissing snakes throw up into the air. It must be caught, so they say, in a cloak before it hits the ground. But you'd better have a horse handy, because the snakes will chase you until they are cut off by some stream. A genuine anguinum will float upstream, even if covered in gold. But as is common with the world's holy men, the Druids say it can only be gathered during a particular phase of the moon, as if people could make the moon and serpents work together. I saw one of these eggs myself—it was a small round thing like an apple with a hard surface full of indentations as on the arms of an octopus. The Druids value them highly. They say it is a great help in lawsuits and will help you gain the good will of a ruler. That this is plainly false is shown by a man of the Gaulish Vocontii tribe, a Roman knight, who kept one hidden in his cloak during a trial before the emperor Claudius and was executed, as far as I can tell, for this reason alone.

"Barbarous rites were found in Gaul even within my own memory. For it was then that the emperor Tiberius passed a decree through the senate outlawing their Druids and these types of diviners and physicians. But why do I mention this about a practice which has crossed the sea and reached the ends of the earth? For even today Britain performs rites with such ceremony that you would think they were the source for the extravagant Persians. It is amazing how distant people are so similar in such practices. But at least we can be glad that the Romans have wiped out the murderous cult of the Druids, who thought human sacrifice and ritual cannibalism were the greatest kind of piety."[22]

In this excerpt, Pliny offers perhaps the richest detail of all of the ancient sources. His account includes details of Druidic ritual - the use of oak groves, the importance of mistletoe - that were not noted anywhere else, and it's perhaps no coincidence that worship in oaken groves was not unique to the Druids, as there is evidence that the Germanic god Thor/Donar was worshiped primarily in this context as well.[23]

Perhaps most importantly, Pliny provides an evocative image that has influenced all later images of the Druids: a white-robed priest with a golden sickle climbing an oak tree to harvest mistletoe while two white bulls bellow on the floor of the grove below.[24] He also notes that the Druids used a lunar calendar that began their months on the fifth day of the lunar cycle and was divided up into months, years and 'ages[25].' The Romans, on the other hand, used a solar calendar that they dated back to the founding of their city ("the Calendar of Romulus"), and a revised form of that calendar is still used across the West today. The existence of a calendar is itself a tribute to the Druids' learning and their ability to not only carefully track celestial motions but also perform relatively complex mathematics; the fact that they apparently did so without writing is even more impressive (though not unique, as the civilizations of the Andes also created elaborate calendars without writing).[26]

The famous Roman historian Livy wrote of a grisly anecdote in the 1st century CE about Celtic sacrifice: "Postumius died there fighting with all his might not to be captured alive. The Gauls stripped him of all his spoils and the Boii took his severed head in a procession to the holiest of their temples. There it was cleaned and the bare skull was adorned with gold, as is their custom. It was used thereafter as a sacred vessel on special occasions and as a ritual drinking-cup by their priests and temple officials." The Romans' grim accounts of human sacrifice were clearly designed to chill the hearts of Roman readers, and scholars might have taken them with a grain of salt except for the fact that they were later confirmed by archaeological evidence.

In total, these written accounts all create a rough outline of the Druids that seems to describe a pan-Celtic order of priests and political functionaries who performed rituals in oak groves using mistletoe. These accounts also suggest the Druids were central to sacred sacrifices, were keepers of a vast body of knowledge (including a calendar) through memorization, especially the theological concept of metempsychosis (the undeath of the soul and reincarnation). Druids also

---

22 *Natural History* by Pliny the Elder, Volume 3, Book XVI: Chapter 95
23 *Thor: The Origins, History and Evolution of the Norse God* by Jesse Harasta (2013). Charles River Editors.
24 A sickle is a hand tool with a handle and a curved blade perhaps as long as a forearm. It was used for harvesting grain and hay.
25 An 'age' here is a roughly defined term, but it may refer to a larger cycle of events akin to the cyclical events in the Mesoamerican Long Count calendar. As the Druids apparently taught about the eternal, yet constantly renewing, nature of the earth, it is possible that Ages were seen as 'restarts' in the celestial cycles.
26 "Mesoamerican Writing Systems" at Ancientscripts.com, accessed online at:
    http://www.ancientscripts.com/ma_ws.html

apparently served as neutral arbitrators and diplomats for the fractious Celtic chiefdoms. The ancient accounts are supported by the weak linguistic evidence that interprets the word "Druid" as originating from term meaning "those who know the oak" and "truth" in Old Celtic.

One of the most important observations that emerges from the Roman accounts is that the Druids had two distinct roles within society, making it all but impossible to completely understand their position among the ancient Celts. On the one hand, they were teachers, ritual leaders and scholars, keeping secret lore. This side is widely recognized in modern writings on the organization. However, the other side of the coin is that the Druids were the diplomats, arbiters and judges of their society, helping to keep the often precarious balance of power and peace between rival chiefdoms and factions in what must have been a complex political environment across ancient Gaul, Britain and Ireland.

The Druids seem to have served as a balancing force by operating as intermediaries between various chiefdoms, and this is probably what Strabo was discussing when he said the Druids "are entrusted with the decision, not only of the private disputes, but of the public disputes as well", to the point that "they even arbitrated cases of war and made the opponents stop when they were about to line up for battle."[27] This role, along with their position as the trusted keepers of wisdom, history and lore, likely ensured that the Druids probably served as a pan-Celtic unifying force in an ever-shifting political landscape. Indeed, there are examples of warring tribal peoples in recent history who share a cultural tradition, with institutions like the Druids that can serve to minimize violence within the group. For example, amongst the Sudanese Nuer people in the 1930s, "leopard skin chiefs" moved between rival villages, negotiating settlements for crimes and cooling hot heads. However, when the Nuer went to war with their neighbors, the Dinka, there was no such institution, and the wars were often much bloodier.[28]

The Roman Occupation

At the time of Julius Caesar's first visit to Britain in 55 BCE, Romans knew very little of this mysterious land, and myths and legends about the fearsome Druids and blue-painted savages abounded in the Roman world. By the late 1st century CE, Britain was securely established within the Roman Empire and becoming an increasingly important and wealthy province that ultimately produced Roman Emperors of its own. The transition from a wild misty backwater into this wealthy addition to the empire was not without difficulty. Rebellions, particularly those staged by the Iceni, were frequent occurrences. The savagery of these rebellions was such that it is difficult to understand how Roman rule was not only preserved, but how the process of Romanization, proven more successful in Britain than in most non-Latin provinces of the empire, was achieved.

---

[27] *The Geography Book IV, Chapter 4:4* by Strabo accessed online at:
http://penelope.uchicago.edu/Thayer/E/Roman/Texts/Strabo/4D*.html#4.4
[28] *The Nuer: A Description of the modes of livelihood and political institutions of a Nilotic People* by E.E. Evans Pritchard (1969 [1940]). Oxford University Press.

The reasons behind this success lie in the nature of the island's political situation, which facilitated a Roman policy of divide and rule. This was used in successful combination with their normal carrot and stick approach to pacifying what, for all intents and purposes, should have been an impossible challenge, seeing as how the Romans were operating so far from their center of power. The Britain invaded by Caesar in 55 BCE was populated by a large number of Iron Age tribes, all of which belonged to a broadly Celtic culture. In the context of Britain, however, the term "Celtic" must be seen as a linguistic one, because despite suggestions of deep-seated cultural links with the Celts of Northern Gaul, there is, in fact, very little evidence of permanent, strong ties between the Celts in Britain and those in Gaul.

The Brythonic language spoken in Britain at this time was similar to that spoken both in Ireland and Gaul, all of which are considered Celtic. Nevertheless, while ongoing links between the various centers of Celtic culture may not have been quite as widespread as earlier scholars had presumed, it is inevitable that people sharing a relatively common language would also share at least some cultural features. Fitzpatrick wrote: "It is clear then, that there is no intrinsic 'Celtic' European unity and that the idea of a Celtic Iron Age Europe has developed in an almost ad hoc fashion. When examined critically, the central idea of being 'Celtic' may also be seen to be weakly formulated."[29] Tacitus believed the Britons to be descendants of migrants from throughout Europe. He concluded the Caledonians were descendants of German settlers, while those in Wales, he argued, came from Iberia, and those in the south from Gaul: "Their physical characteristics are various and this is suggestive, overall however, it seems reasonable to believe that the Gauls occupied this island lying so near to them."[30]

Scholars have long debated the nature of these movements, but whether they were migrations, invasions, or simply a process of "diffusion" is largely unimportant. What matters is that tribes from various parts of the continent did settle in Britain, including the Belgae, who appeared on the island in the 2nd century BCE. Julius Caesar describes this migration in his *Commentaries on the Gallic War,* using the assumed unity of the Belgae and their descendants across the Channel in the war against Rome as the excuse for his invasion in 55 BCE.[31]

There were trading links between the groups in Britain. Archaeological evidence suggests that from the 8th century BCE onward, Celts in Britain traded with their counterparts across the Channel, bringing new ideas on, for example, the manufacture of swords. Trade was not restricted to near neighbors, and evidence confirms that Phoenician traders began visiting the island at about the same time, too, bringing various Mediterranean products with them. Similarly, it is evident that traders from Scandinavia brought their produce to Britain. All of these visitors seemed particularly interested in the country's mineral resources and salt. Goods

---

[29] P. 242, 'Celtic Iron Age Europe: The theoretical basis' by A.P. Fitzpatrick in P. Graves-Brown *Cultural Identity and Archaeology: The Construction of European Communities* (1996). Routledge: London.
[30] Tacitus, *The Life of Cnæus Julius Agricola*, 11.
[31] Julius Caesar, *Commentaries on the Gallic Wars*

were imported from the Hallstatt culture and these, in particular, influenced art in Britain. From the 2nd century BCE onward, Britons made use of trading routes developed by the Romans through Brittany and southwest France to access Italian produce and Hengistbury Head in Dorset became the center for the importation of Italian wine.[32]

Some estimates put the population of Britain in the Iron Age as high as four million by the end of the 1st century BCE, with the greatest density in the southeast. The average life expectancy was around 25-30 years old, although the rates were lower for women due to the many deaths in childbirth. Between 400 BCE and 100 BCE, evidence suggests the development of regional identities, and populations rose steadily, as "growth of population was one of the factors which led to the crystallising out of well-defined social hierarchies accompanied, especially in the south, by a degree of territoriality."[33]

Far from being the painted savages depicted by the Romans, the tribes engaged in extensive trade and commerce. While coinage from around Europe was used for trading purposes by Britons, they also developed and minted their own. Tribal kings put their names on these coins in the continental manner, and there are examples naming, for instance, Tasciovanus from Verulamium and Cunobelinos from Camulodunum. A number of buried hoards have been found throughout England, all confirming both the use of native coinage and the very disparate number of tribes based on specific regional areas.[34]

The Britain that Julius Caesar began taking an interest in from 58 BCE onward was, then, a relatively prosperous land with a large population and numerous, successful—if comparatively small—regionally-based tribes. Caesar's determination to conquer Gaul totally and completely brought his initial attention to those tribes in Britain, based on his assumption they were helping the Gauls in the war against Rome. His underlying focus, however, was always his long-term plan to take total control of Rome. To do that, he had to retain control of his army. To retain that control, he had to have an enemy the Senate perceived to be a real threat to Rome. Therein lies the basis of Caesar's attempts to paint the British, and especially the Druids, as barbarians able to threaten Roman civilisation. The tactics of demonization were not particularly new to the Romans—they had employed the same tactics in the wars against the Carthaginians (who were also accused of being practitioners of human sacrifice). For Caesar, Britain was never an end in itself, but simply a means to with which to attain his greatest objectives, which accounts for his relative lack of success in his invasions compared to his other military exploits. Nevertheless, he brought Britain into the Roman consciousness, and it was inevitable that at some point Rome would turn its full attention to the island.

---

[32] *Greeks Romans and Barbarians: Spheres of Interaction* by B.W. Cunliffe (1988). London.
[33] P. 598, *Iron Age Communities in Britain: An account of England, Scotland and Wales from the Seventh Century BCE until the Roman Conquest, 4th Edition* by B. Cunliffe (2010). Routledge: London.
[34] Coins in Context: coinage and votive deposition in Iron Age South East Leicestershire' by I. Leins (2007). *The British Numismatic Journal* Vol. 77, pp. 2-45.

Andreas Wahra's picture of an ancient bust of Caesar

Caesar's expeditions to Britain in both 55 BCE and 54 BCE have to be viewed against the backdrop of the political situation in Rome at that time. Caesar had control of a large army in Gaul, and his campaign was, to a very large extent, undertaken on the pretext of combating an external threat to the empire. This justified the maintenance of his control over these forces at a time when there was a move in Rome for him to be relieved of his command even before the end of his commission, which was scheduled for 54 BCE.

Thus, Caesar was determined to retain command of his troops at all costs, which was pivotal to his political plans. As outlined in his *Gallic Wars*, he claimed the Britons had been aiding the Gauls and posing a very real threat to the Roman attempt to pacify the newly-conquered country.[35]

The English Channel was generally regarded by the Romans as defining the very edge of the world, and the symbolic significance of crossing the "Ocean" was not lost on Caesar, intent as he was on projecting himself as Rome's greatest general and politician.

The first invasion began in the late summer of 55 BCE, despite the fact that it was already very late in the campaigning season. Gaius Volusenis was sent in a single ship to scout the south coast area as Gaulish merchants had refused to provide any information about Britain to the Romans. He did not land, as "he did not dare leave his ship and entrust himself to the barbarians."[36] The scouting expedition lasted five days and furnished with what little information his tribune had been able to gather, Caesar planned his invasion. Various tribes in the south of Britain grew alarmed as soon as they realized the Romans were intent on invading, and a number of tribes sent envoys to Caesar, offering their submission. He sent these back to the island along with his ally, King Commius of the Atrebates, to win as many tribes over as possible before he landed.

The invasion fleet numbered 80 transport vessels with the capacity to transport the Legio VII, the Legio X, and other fighting ships, and the fleet was assembled at what is now Boulogne, then known as Portus Itius. In addition, Caesar arranged for a further 18 transport ships to take the cavalry from Ambleteuse after he had landed.[37] The fact that Caesar was in something of a hurry is exemplified by the fact he set sail well after midnight on August 23, 55 BCE, without the cavalry, any siege weapons, or any of the baggage assumed necessary for a serious attempt at conquest.[38] This lack of detailed planning has led many historians to conclude that Caesar did not intend the expedition to be one of total subjugation.

Whatever the original aim, it is clear the Romans had initially intended to land at Dover, but upon arrival offshore, the numbers of assembled tribesmen on the cliffs persuaded Caesar that discretion was the better part of valour, and he sailed a further seven miles up the coast to what he thought was an unguarded beach—now thought to be Pegwell Bay on the Island of Thanet—and landed there.[39] The establishment of a beachhead proved extremely difficult, as the British fiercely opposed the landings and were only driven back by ballistae fired from ships anchored off the coast.

A camp was established. Caesar received hostages from the surrounding tribes, but he was unable to consolidate his bridgehead as his cavalry did not arrive. He quickly realized he had not come equipped to deal with a typical (harsh) British winter. Aware of his precarious position,

---

[35] Julius Caesar, *Commentaries on the Gallic Wars*, 4.20. (Trans. by W. A. McDevitte and W. S. Bohn) [Online]. Available at: http://www.forumromanum.org/literature/caesar/gallic_e1.html

[36] Julius Caesar, *Commentaries on the Gallic Wars*, 4.22. (Trans. by W. A. McDevitte and W. S. Bohn) [Online]. Available at: http://www.forumromanum.org/literature/caesar/gallic_e1.html

[37] P. 19, *Britannia: History of Roman Britain* by S. Frere (1987). Routledge: London.

[38] Julius Caesar, *Commentaries on the Gallic Wars*, 4.30. (Trans. by W. A. McDevitte and W. S. Bohn) [Online]. Available at: http://www.forumromanum.org/literature/caesar/gallic_e1.html

[39] Julius Caesar, *Commentaries on the Gallic Wars*, 4.25. (Trans. by W. A. McDevitte and W. S. Bohn) [Online]. Available at: http://www.forumromanum.org/literature/caesar/gallic_e1.html

Caesar decided to return to Gaul rather than risk being stranded in Britain over the winter with the very real possibility of complete defeat. He successfully crossed back to Gaul and continued to receive hostages from two tribes on the southeast of the island. The other tribes, however, believed the threat from Rome to be over and decided not to honor their pledges.

No matter how this particular campaign is assessed—either as an intended invasion or a reconnaissance mission—it failed to achieve any real goals. Despite this, the Senate, awed by the fact that Caesar had gone beyond what they regarded as the "known world", declared a supplication—or thanksgiving—of 20 days in honor of his achievements.

On his return to Gaul, Caesar immediately began to plan for a second invasion, scheduled for 54 BCE. Cicero referred to these plans in letters to a friend, asking him to make sure he acquired a British war chariot for him.[40] The Romans had learned from their mistakes in 55 BCE, and instead of invading with only two Legions, on this occasion, the force was comprised of five plus 2,000 cavalry, and all personnel were carried on ships specially designed for beach landings. He also planned his supply route more carefully and leaving Labienus at Portus Itius to oversee the regular transport of all food and other equipment necessary to maintain an invading force.

The Romans landed at the spot Caesar had identified the previous year, but this time their landing was unopposed. As soon as the bridgehead was established, Caesar ordered Quintus Atrius to advance inland. By the end of the day, this force had covered nearly 12 miles and defeated a British force at Bigbury Wood.[41] The next day, the Romans prepared to march further inland, but a severe storm that wrecked numerous invasion fleet vessels caused Caesar to order his troops back to the coast for repairs.

In early September, Caesar marched inland once again, confronting the forces of Cassivellaunus, the king of a tribe living north of the Thames. Cassivellaunus had recently successfully defeated the Trinovantes and was now their war leader, as well. With a combined force, the Britons harried the Romans but realized they were not strong enough to inflict a decisive defeat on the invaders. Caesar continued his progress northwards, but the constant attacks meant that by the time he had reached the Thames, that one, fordable crossing had been heavily fortified by the Romans who had used an elephant to terrify the Britons and the defenders into abandoning the crossing due to fright.[42] The Trinovantes sent ambassadors promising aid and provisions against Cassivellaunus and the Romans restored Mandubraccius to the Trinovantine throne. Other tribes followed the Trinovantine lead—including the Cenimagni, the Segontiaci, the Ancalites, the Bibroci, and the Cassi—and surrendered. Caesar, now in a more secure position, laid siege to Cassivellaunus' last stronghold at Wheathampstead.[43]

---

[40] Cicero, *Letters to Friends*, 7.6 and 7.7.
[41] P. 22, *Britannia: History of Roman Britain* by S. Frere (1987). Routledge: London.
[42] Polyaenus, *Strategems*, 8.23.5.
[43] P. 25, *Britannia: History of Roman Britain* by S. Frere (1987). Routledge: London.

As in the previous year, Caesar was eager for a resolution to the conflict and was fearful that he would be stranded in Britain over the winter. Consequently, he did not press the siege, and when Cassivellaunus offered to provide tribute and hostages and agree not to attack the Romans' new allies, the Romans agreed to the terms and promptly left the island. No garrison of any sort was left in Britain to enforce the settlement, and it is not known if any tribute was ever paid.[44]

While both of Caesar's two invasions failed to produce military or economic advantages, the second foray provided the Romans with a significant amount of knowledge about the island that they did not have prior to the campaigns. Geographical knowledge was collected, not by Roman advances, but in dealings with local populations. Caesar's discoveries were limited to Kent and the Thames Valley. In his *Commentaries on the Gallic War,* however, Caesar made note that "[t]he climate is more temperate than in Gaul the colds being less severe." He also wrote, "The island is triangular in form and one of its sides is opposite to Gaul. One angle of this side, which is in Kent, whither almost all ships from Gaul are directed, looks to the east. The lower looks to the south. This side extends about 500 miles. Another side lies toward Spain and the west, on which part is Ireland is less, as is reckoned, than Britain, by one half, but the passage from it into Britain is of equal distance with that from Gaul. In the middle of this voyage is an island which is called Mona many smaller islands besides are supposed to lie there, of which islands some have written that at the time of the winter solstice it might be night for thirty consecutive days. We, in our inquiries about the matter ascertained nothing except that, by accurate measurements with water, we perceived the nights to be shorter there than on the continent. The length of this side, as this account states, is 700 miles. The third side is toward north to which portion of the island no land is opposite but an angle of that side looks principally toward Germany. This side is considered to be 800 miles in length. Thus the whole island is about 2,000 miles in circumference."[45]

The actual total circumference of the island, taking account of inlets and so on, is actually about 11,000 miles, but Caesar's figures denoting the approximate shape of the island are extraordinarily accurate. The ability to assess potential landing sites and harbors proved invaluable in the next century.

Caesar was also able to assess the Britons, informing Roman attitudes from that point onward. He explained, "The interior of Britain is inhabited by those of whom they say that it is handed down by tradition that they were born in the island itself. The maritime portion by those who had passed over from the country of the Belgae for the purpose of plunder and war, almost all of whom are called by the names of those states from which being sprung they went thither and having waged war continued there and began to cultivate the lands. The number of people is countless and their buildings exceedingly numerous for the most part very like those of Gaul. They do not regard it lawful to eat the hare, and the cock and the goose, they do, however, breed

---

[44] Caesar, *Letters to Atticus*, 5.
[45] Caesar, *Letters to Atticus*, 5.13.

them for amusement and pleasure."[46]

Caesar concluded that the most civilized of the British tribes were those living in Kent, though he noted the Britons did not sow corn but tended to live on milk and flesh instead. He confirmed all of the tribes used blue woad to decorate themselves for war, wore their hair long, and used animal skins for clothing. He was intrigued by the custom of their shaving every part of their bodies except for the hair and upper lip, and even more fascinated by the practice of sharing up to a dozen wives between warriors. The father of any child born from such unions was, he recorded, always assumed to be that of the first husband.[47]

Caesar was also able to study British military tactics, and he provided details about chariot warfare, which was a specialty of the British: "Firstly they drive about in all directions and throw their weapons and generally break the ranks of the enemy with the very dread of their horses and the noise of their wheels and when they have worked themselves in between the troops of horse, leap from their chariots to engage on foot. The charioteers in the meantime withdraw some little distance from the battle and so place themselves with the chariots that if their masters are overpowered by the number of the enemy they may have a ready retreat to their own troops. Thus they display in battle the speed of horse, together with the firmness of infantry and by daily practice and exercise, attain to such expertness that they are accustomed, even on a declining and steep place to check their horses at full speed and manage and turn them in an instant and run along the pole and stand on the yoke, and thence betake themselves with the greatest celerity to their chariots again."[48]

Caesar undoubtedly respected the Britons' military attributes and even copied a style of boat he had seen on the island during the subsequent civil war he fought against Pompey years later.[49] He was less enthusiastic about the Druidic religion—which he believed originated in Britain—going so far as to claim the Druids in Gaul had all been trained there.[50] He also appreciated the economic potential of the island and was convinced it would be a valuable addition to the Roman Empire: "The number of cattle is great. They use either brass or iron rings, determined at a certain weight, as their money. Tin is produced in the midland regions in the maritime, iron…there is timber of every description."[51]

Caesar did not conquer Britain, but what he did do—especially by restoring Mandubracius to the Trinovantine throne—was begin the system of client kingdoms. In so doing, he brought the island within the Roman orbit. One of his most significant successes, although perhaps only realized retrospectively in 43 CE, was that he established alliances with key kings. Trading links

---

[46] Caesar, *Letters to Atticus*, 5.12.
[47] Caesar, *Letters to Atticus*, 5.14.
[48] Caesar, *Letters to Atticus*, 4.33.
[49] Caesar, *Letters to Atticus*, 1.54.
[50] Caesar, *Letters to Atticus*, 6.13.
[51] Caesar, *Letters to Atticus*, 5.2.

also developed significantly over the coming years.

Caesar's contribution to the eventual conquest of Britain is best summed up by Tacitus: "It was, in fact, the divine Julius who first of all Romans entered Britain with an army, he overawed the natives by a successful battle and made himself master of the coast, but it may be said that he revealed, rather than bequeathed, Britain to Rome."[52]

From Caesar's second invasion in 54 BCE to Emperor Claudius's invasion nearly 100 years later, the status quo between Rome and Britain—involving hostages and tribute—was maintained without direct military occupation of the island. Caesar's presumptive heir, Octavian, prepared to invade in 34 BCE, 27 BCE, and 25 BCE, but two of these dates were abandoned due to pressing problems elsewhere in the empire and the third was preempted because the British tribes came to terms with Rome.[53]

---

[52] Tacitus, *The Life of Cnæus Julius Agricola*, 13.
[53] Dio Cassius, *Roman History*, 49.38.

An ancient statue of Augustus

Strabo reflected on Augustus' policy toward Britain during this period, concluding it was founded on pure pragmatism: "And for the purposes of political power, there would be no advantage in knowing such distant countries and their inhabitants, particularly where the people live in islands which are such that they can neither injure or benefit us in any way, because of their isolation. For although the Romans could have possessed Britain, they scorned to do so, for they saw that there was nothing at all to fear from Britain, since they are not strong enough to cross over and attack us. No corresponding advantages would arise by taking over and holding the country. For at present more seems to accrue from the customs duties on their commerce than direct taxation could supply, if we deduct the cost of maintaining an army to garrison the island and collect the tribute. The unprofitableness of an occupation would be still more marked in the case of the other islands near Britain."[54]

---

[54] Strabo, *Geography*, 2.5.8.

The next potential invasion of Britain was led by Caligula in 40 CE, initially reported on by Suetonius and then Dio Cassius, who recounted the story of Caligula collecting huge amounts of sea shells and declaring this the tribute he had won from Neptune. "Having secured these spoils for it was evident that he needed booty for his triumphal procession, he became greatly elated, as if he had subdued the Ocean itself. He gave many presents to his soldiers. He took back the shells to Rome in order to exhibit his booty there as well."[55]

Louis le Grand's picture of a bust of Caligula

By 40 CE, the political situation in Britain was in turmoil due to the emergence of the Catevellauni as the most powerful tribe. They displaced Rome's allies, the Trinovantes, which prompted Rome to consider invasion. It is not known what made Caligula decide to abandon his invasion plans, though he certainly took steps that aided Claudius three years later. Most notably, it was under Caligula that the Romans built a lighthouse at what is now Boulogne, a structure that stood until the 16th century.

Dio Cassius wrote extensively on the real invasion, which began in 43 CE. From his work, it is known that the invasion force was led by Aulus Plautius, the distinguished senator, and

---

[55] Dio Cassius, *Roman History*, 59, 25.1.3.

comprised four legions, one of which was commanded by Vespasian, the future emperor. The army assembled at Boulogne, crossing over to Britain in three phases and apparently landing at Richborough on the east coast of Kent. Richborough had a large, natural harbor, and excavations do seem to confirm this was the landing place. That said, some historians argue the landing place was in the vicinity of Noviomagus, Chichester, in territory formerly ruled by Verica. Ostensibly, the invasion had taken place to restore Verica as ruler.[56]

British resistance to the Romans was more organized than in the time of Caesar and was led by two formidable commanders, Togodumnus and Caratacus, son of Cunobeline, King of the Catevellauni. The two armies met near Rochester on the River Medway, and after two days of intense fighting, the Romans emerged victorious. The Britons retreated to the Thames, where Togodumnus was killed. Caratacus evaded capture, however, and fled to the west to continue his resistance against the Romans.

Aulus Plautius was, he believed, assured of victory and sent for Claudius to join him for the final push. Dio Cassius claimed Aulus Plautius sent for Claudius because he needed the emperor to secure the victory: "On receiving his message Claudius committed affairs in Rome including the command of the troops to his fellow consul Lucius Vitellius, whom he had kept in office, like himself, for the full half year and set out for Britain...Taking over the command of the troops in Britain himself he crossed the Thames and engaged the barbarians who had assembled to oppose him. He defeated them and captured Camulodunum, the capital of Cunobelinus. After this he won over a number of tribes some by diplomacy some by force and was saluted as Imperator several times, contrary to precedent."[57]

Claudius was certainly no military man, and on his triumphal arch in Rome, it is claimed that Claudius received the surrender of 11 kings without any losses. In *Twelve Caesars*, Suetonius states that Claudius received the surrender of the Britons without battle or bloodshed.[58] It is more likely that by the time Claudius arrived, the Britons had, in effect, been beaten, so the elephants and heavy war engines brought by Claudius were superfluous. They would, however, have presented an imposing spectacle for Claudius's march to Camulodunum, where the Romans had established their new capital.

Despite having had very little to do with the actual defeat of the Britons, Claudius milked the victory for all it was worth. Dio Cassius noted, "The Senate on hearing of his achievements voted him the title Britannicus, and gave him permission to hold a triumph. They also voted an annual festival to commemorate the event and decreed that two triumphal arches should be erected, one in Rome and one in Gaul, since it was from Gaul that he had crossed over into Britain. They bestowed on his son the same title and indeed in a way Britannicus came to be the

---

[56] Strabo, *Geography*, 4.5.2.
[57] Dio Cassius, *Roman History*, 60.19.1-21.5.
[58] Suetonius, *Life of Claudius*, 17.

boy's usual name."[59]

Marie-Lan Nguyen's picture of a bust of Claudius

Vespasian pursued Caratacus west and set up a legionary base at Exeter. While this was going on, the Legio IX was sent north and established a Roman center at Lincoln.

Josephus seemingly exaggerated Vespasian's role in the conquest of Britain, claiming it had been he who had added Britain to the empire, "and thus provided Claudius, the father of Nero, with a triumph which cost him no personal exertion."[60] Regardless of whoever was most responsible, within only four years of the invasion, the area south of a line from the Humber to the Severn estuary was under Roman control.

Roman consolidation of their new province continued apace under the new Governor Publius Ostorius Scapula who, in 47 CE, began a campaign against the Welsh tribes.

Key to the Roman success was their defeat of Caratacus whom they bested in the Battle of

---

[59] Dio Cassius, *Roman History*, 60.22.1-23.6.
[60] Josephus, *The Wars of the Jews*, 3.1.2(4).

Caer Caradoc. He sought sanctuary with the Brigantes, whose queen, Cartimandua, promptly handed him over to her Roman allies. His wife and daughter were already in Roman hands, having been captured after the battle. Tacitus described Caratacus in fairly glowing terms, writing, "The natural ferocity of the inhabitants was intensified by their belief in the prowess of Caratacus whose many undefeated battles and even many victories had made him pre-eminent among British chieftains. His deficiency in strength was compensated by superior cunning and topographical knowledge. Transferring the war to the country of the Ordovices he was joined by everyone who found the prospect of a Roman peace alarming."[61]

Tacitus recalls that Caratacus was held in some esteem in Rome despite nine years of warfare, and although he was paraded through Rome as a prisoner, Claudius pardoned his erstwhile foe after he had made a noble speech to the Senate. He may have lived the remainder of his life in the city.

The defeat of Caratacus was not, however, the end of the disturbances in Britain, and further trouble erupted with the Silures and the Brigantes. Ostorius died shortly after Caratacus's defeat and was succeeded by Aulus Didius Gallus, who, upon his arrival in Britain, found that a Roman brigade under Manlius Valens had suffered a reversal. The whole incident was magnified, for various reasons, by both sides in an internal struggle between Brigantine factions. Having resolved that issue, Gallus turned his attention to the consolidation of Roman gains in Wales. Nero became Emperor in 54 CE, and he was keen to expand the invasion even further north. He appointed Quintus Veranius as governor, and he and his successor, Gaius Suetonius Paulinus, extended Roman control in Wales, destroying the seat of Druidical power on Mona, present-day Anglesey, in 60 CE.

The Romans seem to have had an almost pathological hatred of the Druids since the days of Julius Caesar, and this sentiment was shared by Claudius. It was the determination to exterminate them that led to a significant part of the Roman forces in Britain being in the north when Boudica's revolt erupted.

The reason for the intensity of this antipathy towards the Druids is difficult to fathom, as all the evidence available suggests the individuals that were called Druids seem to have been high-ranking members of a professional class that served Celtic society. They were, of course, religious leaders, but they also served as legal authorities, lore keepers, doctors, and political advisers. They were thought to have been literate, but they were prevented by their doctrine from recording their knowledge in any written form. They left no written accounts of themselves or their beliefs. Consequently, the modern understanding of what they did and who they were comes only from the Greek and Roman sources.

The major philosophy of the Druids centered on the immortality of the soul: "The Pythagorean

---

[61] Tacitus, *The Annals*, 12.31-3.

doctrine prevails among the Gauls' teaching that the souls of men are immortal and that after a fixed number of years they will enter into another body." [62] Caesar noted, "With regard to their actual course of studies the main object of all education is, in their opinion, to imbue their scholars with a firm belief in the indestructability of the human soul which according to their belief merely passes at death from one tenement to another, for by such doctrine alone, they say, which robs death of all its terrors, can the highest form of human courage be developed. Subsidiary to the teachings of this main principle, they hold various lectures and discussions on astronomy, on the extent and geographical distribution of the globe, on the different branches of natural philosophy and on many problems connected with religion."[63]

There does not appear to be too much in the Druid philosophy as understood by the Romans at the time that should have caused them undue concern. Nevertheless, it did.

Whether the Romans believed the Celtic idea of immortality would imbue them with no fear of death, thus making them more effective weapons of war, is not known. It's also possible that the influence the Druids had over the local kings was seen as a barrier to Roman attempts to manipulate local leaders or whether the Druidical aversion to bribery marked them for special treatment is a matter of conjecture. What is clear is that Roman leaders took every possible step to exterminate the Druids throughout the Celtic world. Their efforts were ultimately so successful that by the end of the 1st century CE, there is little evidence of any Druids still practicing their religion, but it would all come at a great cost, instigating a large rebellion that threatened to push the Romans out of the region altogether.

---

[62] Alexander Cornelius Polyhistor.
[63] Julius Caesar, *Gallic Wars*, VI.13.

Boudica's Background

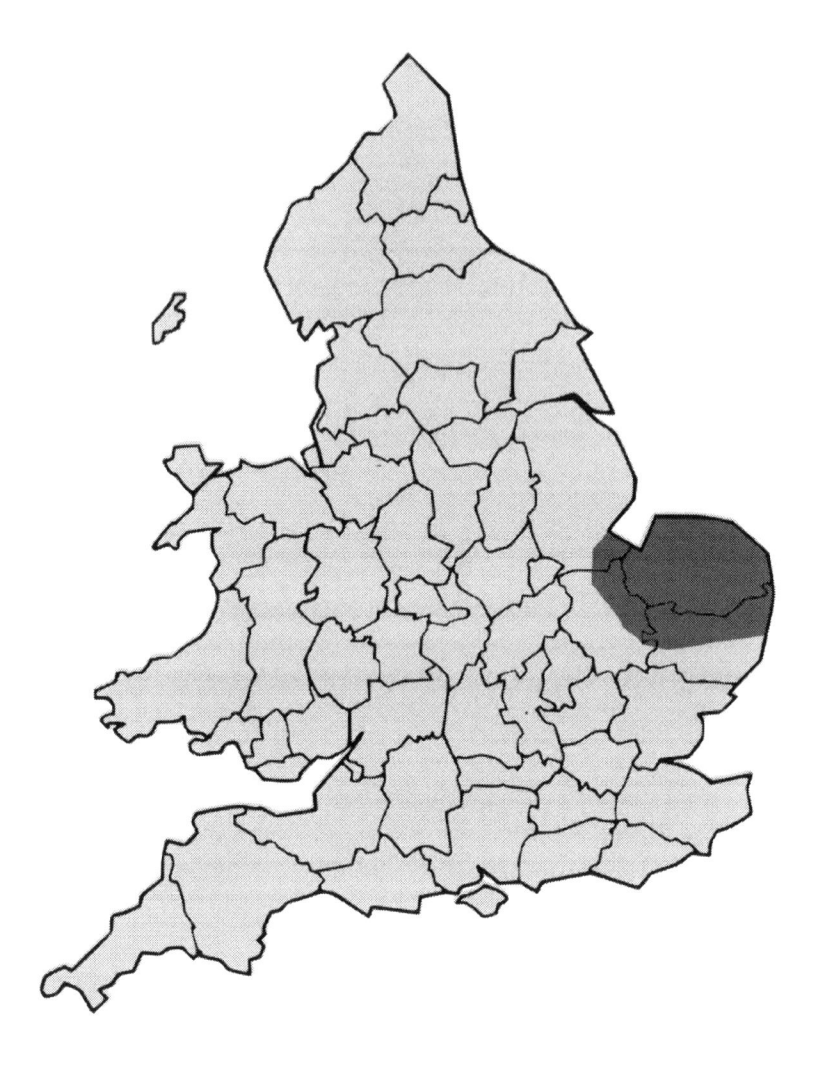

A map of Iceni territory in ancient Britain

    When Boudica was coming of age in the 1st century CE, her people tilled the soil, grew wheat and barley, and raised their sheep and oxen upon the sleepy hillsides. Due to the heavy rainfall, dikes and ditches were constructed by the indigenous people to raise their dwellings above the water table and provide pasturage to raise their livestock. Their thatched roundhouses, made of wood, had a central fire with holes through the roofs to allow the smoke to exit. Even so, the houses were smoky and cold in the winter, and sometimes, several heads of horses or cattle were brought inside to provide heat. Naturally, sanitation was a challenge, particularly in the harsh winters of the British Isles. The door always opened toward the rising sun according to their religious mythology, that of the ancient Druids.

Boudica and her family were of the Iceni tribe, a group of Celts who settled in what was later named East Anglia. The Iceni were located where the province of Norfolk and part of Suffolk are today. The area had many marshes and many iron bogs, so it was a rich source of iron used for tools, weapons, and armor. The Iceni warriors wore animal skins and carried spears, but through trade with the Phoenicians, they learned how to fashion short swords and other weapons.

From 300 BCE until the 1st century CE, deforestation occurred because the Celts desperately needed the land cleared for their sheep, oxen, and horses. The scenic farmsteads were open in those days, unlike nearby communities, and each extended family or tribe was protected by the royalty in the inner dwelling.

Iceni women were unlike the women in Europe. Although they did not normally serve in a military capacity, they worked the farms right along with the farmers, including royals. As a result, Boudica would frequently remove her ceremonial robes and jewelry and work the land as well, helping build her into a tough and strong woman.

For defense, the Celts built hill fortresses, the remains of which can still be found today, and they used spears, shields, knives, and daggers in battle, whether against tribal rivals or beasts like the wild boars which ferreted in their fields for food and fiercely attacked them. They covered themselves in blue dye ahead of conducting battle, and this blue dye, called "Woad," was made from the leaves of a common yellow flower that grew in the area. The belief was that this made them different in appearance, which it certainly did, and it was believed to be a sign of courage. The Romans would initially be taken back by their appearance, but given that Roman soldiers were clad in heavily segmented armor and had helmets, the Celts would find themselves at a severe disadvantage.

Boudica's parents, Diras and Locrinus, were of royal descent, and there are many varieties of the spelling of Boudica's name, including Bonduca, Boudicea, Boudica or Boudicca. The name in Celtic means "Victory," and medieval historians drew a parallel between her and the Arthurian Legends. Like Boudica, the legendary King Arthur was a Celt, and his father was named Uther Pendragon. The name "Uther" is linguistically related to "Victor," the female form of which is "Victoria." The Latin equivalent of that is "Boudicca."

Like her people, she loved the land, which yielded not only fine grasses for sheep grazing but gold, iron, and silver. Reportedly lovely and alluring, Boudica was adorned with braided gold necklaces, torc neck ornaments, earrings, rings, and carefully designed bracelets. Boudica's family encouraged the Iceni people to keep their jewelry in "hoards," or caches placed in pottery and buried, and these would later provide bribes for invaders in order to preserve the lives of the people. Some of those items make up what is known as the "Snettisham Treasure," one of the largest collections of Iron Age artifacts unearthed by archeologists in Northwest Norfolk in 1948.

Examples of the torc necklace that Boudica reportedly wore were among the finely crafted jewelry found in that trove.

The Iceni minted coins of gold and silver, and these coins were impressed with animal images, including a boar and a horse. Archeologists have found as many as 15,000 silver coins in 36 different styles, and it seems the Iceni used these to buy goods from nearby tribes of Celts such as the Segontiaci, Trinovantes, the Ancalites, the Brigantes, the Dumnonii, and the Cassi. The Iceni people were clearly more advanced than the Romans described, with a carefully delineated culture, a currency exchange system, a judicial system, a government, and records of their history.

The Celts believed in making peace whenever possible and were open to the arrival of other cultures to their land. This is likely because they consisted of people escaping the Roman domination in Gaul, and many of these tribes from Northern Gaul intermarried with the local population. Together they were called the Gallo-Belgic tribes, with "Belgic" being a term similar to "Belgium," later established in that mainland area. Gallo-Belgic coins discovered in that area date back as early as 100 BCE.

Some of the seafaring Celts lived in the areas near present-day Kent, where five rounded mounds date back to the Iron Age and serve as one of the area's many tourist sites. Furthermore, evidence of six defensive systems with ditches has been found and is believed to be the remnants of the Iceni hill fortress. In the 1970s, aerial surveillance located what came to be called "Boadicea's Palace." It is a square ditch enclosure with suggestions of buildings within, and the structures are located near what is today called Thetford Castle Hill.

Caesar himself described the Iceni in his writings, calling them the "Cenimagni," and they would leave a legacy that affected how Britons viewed the Celts centuries later. In 540 CE, an old monk by the name of Gildas called Boudica a "deceitful lioness" and called the Iceni people "crafty foxes." Gildas thought of Boudica as just another "rebel" who would not submit herself and her people to the Romans, characterizations that make clear the Christian monk despised the Celtic beliefs.

The Iceni were clever enough to know how to deal with people who threatened to overpower them in war. As such, they sent hostages, made agreements and treaties, and promised tributes of precious metals and agricultural products to the Romans. The Romans couldn't help but notice the gold Iceni jewelry, and eventually the Iceni's tribal lands became client states for Rome, in the form of small kingdoms which paid tribute to Rome. That said, Roman historians noted the Iceni never paid the stiff tribute Caesar demanded. In general, the Romans considered the Celts (and Picts) as primitive "barbarians," but Caesar conceded, "By far the most civilized are those living in Kent (a purely maritime district) …Most of the tribes of the interior do not grow corn but live on milk and meat and wear skins."

During the invasion under Claudius, the Celtic tribes offered little resistance to the Romans who entered the areas near Kent south of the Thames River, mostly because they were so frequently at war with each other that they overlooked this new Roman threat. To keep the peace and maintain healthy trade relations, many Celts rekindled the friendly relations with the Romans as some had in Caesar's time.

One of the tribal kings at this time was the Iceni King Prasutagus, Boudica's husband. Prasutagus was familiar with the strength of the Romans and their formidable weapons, and he wanted peace for his people, so he bent to the Roman yoke and got along so well with the Roman overlords that he even attained Roman citizenship. He also accepted a considerable loan from Claudius and used it to help the Iceni. The Roman statesman Seneca even supplemented that with yet another loan. Claudius liked Prasutagus enough that the emperor ended up being lenient when it came to collecting on that loan. He received many favors from Boudica's husband for the sake of peace.

Celtic Resistance

Young Boudica had heard tales about the Romans who had invaded earlier, so she was ambivalent. Furthermore, she was concerned about her husband's obsequious treatment of Claudius. Like Prasutagus, most of the tribes were afraid to resist the mighty armies of Rome and contented themselves with paying tribute and maintaining a light trade, but some Celtic groups were not so complacent. They surreptitiously hid in the forests of the highlands and secret places in the swamps, likely hoping that the Romans would find little of interest in this deserted wetland in the south of Britain and would sail back home as they did once before. That did not happen this time, especially not after the new governor of the region, Plautius, heard reports about Togodumnus and Caractacus, two rebellious tribal leaders whose tribes had defied Rome during Caesar's invasion. According to that information, the two tribes had occupied the area around the Thames River and were a seafaring people who had a brisk trade with Gaul. Catuvellauni was the strongest Celtic leader in the area and was called king by the population of Celts who lived there. Togodumnus led the tribe known as the Trinovantes, and their antipathy toward Rome was the same then as in Caesar's time.

Plautius commissioned his legions to slaughter Togodumnus and Caractacus, and eventually they ferreted out Togodumnus' people. The Romans attacked him and his troops with broadswords and arrows, and the superior arms of the Romans forced him to retreat.

For the time being, the Roman commander, Aulus Plautius, made no ostensibly aggressive moves except to seek out those who were loyal to Togodumnus and Caractacus. The Trinovantes and the Catuvellauni Celts became alarmed and spread the Woad dye upon their skin and shaven heads as they gathered their horses and war chariots in the area. Plautius then dispatched the formidable warrior, Flavius Vespasian, and Sabinus, who marched north toward the Thames.

When attempting to cross the river waters, some of the less experienced Romans hesitated because of the depth of the tidal lakes that had formed during the tide, but the Germanic mercenaries they brought with them were expert swimmers and forged across the Thames, brandishing their broadswords. Once they crossed, the Germans fought on behalf of Rome and slashed the Trinovantes and the Catuvellauni rebels right and left. Their javelins and arrows rained down, killing both men and horses, and in the heat of battle, the courageous Celtic leader Togodumnus was killed as he stood on top of his chariot on the opposite side of the River Thames. The battle lasted two long days, but the Romans prevailed and many Celts were slaughtered and lay bleeding in the waters of the River Thames, turning it red.

In the meantime, Plautius remained south of the Thames with his main force, hesitant to cross because some of the Roman soldiers were afraid of these "blue-dyed barbarians," as he called them. Word had it that those warriors knew no fear. Plautius was eventually succeeded by Publius Ostorius Scapula, who sought out the other missing Celtic firebrand, Caractacus. Scapula split his forces into groups, and when one of the groups was confronted with a wandering rebel force of Celts, the Roman cavalry attacked. This attack ended up being unsuccessful because of the thick woods.

Scapula determined that what he needed was a legion to block access to the Severn River at a bridge. Scapula also managed to kidnap Caractacus's wife and daughters, compelling Caractacus's brothers to surrender, but Caractacus himself fled to the land of the Brigantes tribe. Later on, the queen of the Brigantes, Cartimandua, revealed the location of Caractacus to the Romans. A personification of Cartimandua's name means "sleek filly," and that was hardly a compliment, as she was reportedly licentious, unbridled, corrupt and used her feminine wiles to get what she wanted. Considered an evil leader who betrayed the Celtic cause, when she divorced her husband Venutius, he raised an army against her, and as retribution, Cartimandua had his entire family killed.

As a result of Cartimandua's betrayal, the Romans knew the general location where Caractacus was, and they pursued him. Tacitus wrote, "Caractacus resorted to the ultimate hazard, adopting a place for battle so that entry, exit, everything would be unfavorable to us and for the better to his own men, with steep mountains all around, and, wherever a gentle access was possible, he strewed rocks in front in the manner of a rampart. And in front too there flowed a stream with an unsure ford, and companies of armed men had taken up position along the defenses."

The Romans chased him all the way to Wales, and they finally captured Caractacus in the aftermath of the Battle of Caer Caradoc. Caractacus was taken to Rome, where he was paraded as a prisoner and made to appear before the Roman Senate. However, Caractacus awed them with his courage and eloquence, telling the Roman officials, "If you wish to command everyone, does it really follow that everyone should accept your slavery? If I were now being handed over as one who had surrendered immediately, neither my fortune nor your glory would have achieved brilliance."

Caractacus lived out his life in Rome and became a respected figure there, setting the example that peace between people could be achieved if the incoming forces made an effort to understand and appreciate the culture and beliefs of the natives. Shakespeare would go on to use Caractacus as inspiration for one of the characters in the play *Cymbeline*.

For her part, Boudica was distressed when she heard the news of Romans infiltrating the capital of Camulodunum (now the modern city of Colchester on the southeastern coast of England). Claudius's forces had arrived in Britain with a troop of frightful elephants and constructed a fortress and garrison at the capital city, coercing many of the local Celtic men to aid in its construction. Celts were also made to serve as slaves and swordsmen. While some were old and infirm, others were still quite capable of doing battle, and according to Tacitus, the barracks in the town of Camulodunum was "a strong colony of ex-soldiers established on conquered territory to provide a protection against rebels and a center for instructing the provincials in the procedures of the law." The town was then renamed "Colonia Victricensis," meaning "triumph."

When Boudica was around the age of 19, one of the greatest insults suffered by the Celts took place. A temple was erected to Emperor Claudius at Camulodunum, a literal representation of the fact Claudius had earned the term "Britannicus" back in Rome as the ruler of the British Isles. The temple in this city was intended to demonstrate his superiority locally and heighten his reputation back home.

The temple had a colonnade of pillars that were over three feet in diameter, and eagles – the symbols of Rome – adorned the top of each column. This temple was intended to inspire a feeling of appreciation and awe into the hearts of the Britons, but it was an indignity instead. To make this truly a Roman site, beautiful stone tombs were also built for the Roman veterans of the British campaigns, while Celtic places of worship in the city were destroyed. A great statue to Victoria, the Roman goddess of victory, was erected near the temple, and the Romans even coerced a few of the Celts to serve as priests for the temple, requiring them to spend what gold and silver they had to perform elaborate religious ceremonies for the occupying Romans. The Druid priests were no longer respected like they were when Caesar was there, so they were dismissed or tortured and killed. The Claudian temple served as a constant symbol of occupation.

Making things more precarious, there was also a Roman fortress built to house Legion XX. It was surrounded by a ditch to discourage entry by rebels, and the entire settlement was enclosed by a wall. Archeologists found skulls in the ditch around the fort with sword cuts, possibly the remains of Druids or other Celts.

All the extravagances of the Roman society could be found in Camulodunum. They had bathhouses, a theater, and gardens adorned with sculptures of the Roman gods. Celts were made to act as servants and wait upon the Roman administrators, and some of the tribal territories yielded to a *civitas* system. The *civitas* was essentially a town center with some of the native Celtic royalty participating in governance but ruled by a provincial governor from Rome who had a procurator functioning as a tax collector. Taxes were collected from the people and forwarded to the Roman military and administration.

After the death of Claudius, some of the Celts continued to subject themselves to the Romans and were Romanized, and those who did so ran the provinces. One of them was Prasutagus, then leading the Iceni. Thus, when Prasutagus married Boudica around the year 49 CE, he was the king, and he subsequently became the Roman governor of the Iceni territory. He and Boudica lived a peaceful existence, but clearly Boudica resented this governmental change and its impact on the Celts.

Omens

One day, the Roman people were alarmed by women who claimed to have awakened during a visionary dream. They saw the Roman statue of Victory at the Temple of Claudius turn backward and be hurled to the ground. Bloodied bodies lay all around, and the tributaries ran red with blood. Like the Celts, the Romans were accustomed to divinations, and it was said in those early days that the Roman women prophesied about the impending destruction that was about to befall the occupying Romans in Britain. They had visions of ghostly figures of dead men wandering about in their marketplace in Camulodonum.

These visions coincided with the rise of the notorious Emperor Nero, who succeeded Claudius in 54 CE. Caesar had essentially conquered Southern Britain, and Claudius had occupied Central Britain, Southern Britain, and some small areas of modern-day Wales, but most of the north remained untouched. The Picts and Scots were among the tribes in the Highlands, and the Romans naturally craved the whole land.

When Nero became the new emperor in Rome, Prasutagus, sought to make himself and his people well-known and respected under Nero's new administration, but that would not happen. Though he tried to appease Emperor Nero with gifts and praise, Prasutagus was virtually ignored, and Nero dispatched more Roman troops to the area.

The Iceni also had another problem. The Roman general, Gaius Suetonius Paulinus, who was the father of the famed historian of that era, Gaius Suetonius Tranquillas, had made large loans to these Iceni Celts to assure that they would send shipments of crops from their fields. Now that Nero headed the Roman Empire, Suetonius Paulinus felt he had enough military support to exact payment on those loans or force the Iceni who could not pay to forfeit their land. Prasutagus knew nothing of these plans and wanted to preserve peace for his people and protection of their fertile farmlands. In his will, he left some of the government-controlled lands to Emperor Nero, his throne to his wife, and the land to his daughters.

At this time, Rome did not recognize female heirs of a kingdom. According to Livy, the Romans did not believe a woman could rule, and in general they were looked upon by Romans as deceitful and self-centered, more attentive toward their appearance, clothing, and jewelry than they would be toward governing a kingdom. Romans also felt that women lust power and would even compromise their beliefs and morality to achieve it.

Thus, when Prasutagus died in the year 60 CE, the Romans virtually ignored his will, making Boudica's role and that of her two female children tenuous.

In part due to the fact Claudius's actions indicated the Romans had comprehensively pacified Britain, Nero was emboldened to take a firmer stance there. At the same time, his military commander, Gaius Suetonius Paulinus, prodded him into conquering the Iceni for the money they owed to Rome. Seneca, who had also provided loans, was previously Nero's tutor and remained close to the emperor, so his influence in the affairs of Britain was strong.

Throughout this time, the Romans looked down upon them as inferior people and developed a cavalier attitude toward them. In his annals, the historian Nennius wrote that "by land there was no marshalled army, no right wing of battle, nor other preparation for resistance but their backs were their shields against their vanquishers, and presented their necks to the swords, while chill terror ran through every limb and they stretched out their hands to be bound, like women: so that is has become a proverb far and wide, that the Britons are neither brave in war, nor faithful in times of peace."

It was alleged that on one occasion, when Boudica approached the Romans and complained about their behavior, they grabbed her, fastened her arms to a post, and viciously scourged her. It was also alleged that soldiers raped Boudica's daughters repeatedly, a brutally physical way of demonstrating their power over her and making her subservient. They flogged her in public to terrify the masses, but as it turned out, Boudica and the Iceni would not be deterred. After they lashed Boudica, Druid priestesses and Iceni women carefully carried her into one of their huts and nursed her wounds.

Anglesey is an island off the coast of North Wales and is the largest island in the Irish Sea. The Welsh term for Anglesey is *Ynys Mon*, hence it was also called "Mona." Anglesey was the homeland of the Druids, and Anglesey was also a place of refuge for those fleeing Roman oppression in the tribal areas. It had many natural groves of yew trees, along with oaks which the Druids held sacred. Both were considered to be the trees of the spirits, and the Druids kept altars there and nursed the holy groves of yew trees along with the sacred oaks.

To achieve mastery over Anglesey, Nero appointed his most capable general, Suetonius Paulinus, governor of the island. Suetonius was obsessed with competing against other accomplished Roman generals throughout the empire, so he felt pressure to impress the emperor. That made targeting this land of the Druids, which had a high mountain and enormous troves of copper, an ideal idea. The island would also serve as a lookout where Romans could keep watch over Ireland to the west.

By this time, the Romans had learned how to build flat-bottomed boats to navigate the shallower waters of inland Britain, and in places where the water was deep, the cavalry swam alongside their horses. In great numbers, the Roman swift boats invaded Anglesey, but as Suetonius was landing, his army was frightened by the appearance of black-robed Druid women with wild hair. They called out to their gods to rescue them, while around them were robed priests with hands lifted to the sky shouting words and chants. The Druids of Mona were not trained militarily, so they had to invoke what divine powers they could.

To frighten the Romans, they held up lighted torches marked with insignias and cried to the heavens. According to Tacitus, "In the style of Furies, in robes of deathly black and with disheveled hair, they brandished their torches; while a circle of Druids, lifting their hands to heaven and showering imprecations, struck the troops with such an awe at the extraordinary spectacle that, as though their limbs were paralyzed, they exposed their bodies to wounds without an attempt at movement." On the ground below were altars covered with the blood of their victims (mostly animals), from whose entrails divinations were made.

Suetonius calmed his men and called out to his soldiers. He used the mercenary forces of Batavia to lead a surprise vanguard attack carried out with amphibious vessels. They destroyed the Druid shrine there and their sacred groves of yews, and then they burned the fields and crops. Legions of the newly conscripted Iceni Celts were forced to fight the Druids along with the Romans, so they rushed headlong into the Druids and people of the land of Mona. After the assault, the Roman centurions slaughtered much of the population.

This Roman intrusion was not only a physical but a sacrilegious attack. Boudica was a Druid who had a link to the divine gods of the Celtic religion, so naturally, she and the Iceni were livid when they heard about the attack.

Boudica's Revolt

The final subjugation of Wales and the suppression of the Druids had to be deferred in 60 CE because the Romans had to turn their attention to the biggest threat to their invasion since 43 CE: the revolt of the Iceni.

While the death of Prasutagus and the subsequent treatment of his wife and daughters was undoubtedly a major factor in the Iceni rebellion, the whole uprising had more deep-seated causes. Tacitus recorded, "Prasutagus, King of the Iceni, after a life of long and renowned prosperity, had made the emperor co-heir with his own two daughters. Prasutagus hoped by this submissiveness to reserve his kingdom and household from attack. But it turned out otherwise. After his death, the kingdom and household alike were plundered like prizes of war, the one by

Roman officers the other by Roman slaves. As a beginning his widow Boudicca was flogged and their daughters raped. The Icenian chiefs were deprived of their hereditary estates as if the Romans had been given the whole country. The king's own relatives were treated like slaves and the humiliated Iceni feared still worse now that they had been reduced to provincial status. So they rebelled."[64]

The Iceni had rebelled in 47 BCE, and it appears that Prasutagus had been put onto the throne by the Romans as a way of keeping control of the area. The terms of Prasutagus's will, it is suggested, were constructed in such a way as to help his daughters continue his policy of cooperation with Rome and thereby sideline Boudica.[65] If so, it would not work.

Boudicca seized the opportunity presented by her own ill-treatment and that of her daughters to begin another revolt against the Romans. The trouble quickly spread to the Trinovantes, who had their own grievances against Rome. Britons felt generally angry at the establishment of Rome's imperial cult, which was, of course, specifically intended to impress the natives with the might and majesty of both Rome and the emperor, as well as to act as the focal point for loyalty. The Romans used the cult in a number of ways, including enrolling the local aristocracy as priests, thus involving them in Roman public life. The intention was to Romanize the class of natives that would become the governing class, and who would then undertake the burden of running and administering the province in Rome's interests.

The attempt misfired badly, and the spark of rebellion created by Boudicca's treatment quickly lit fires elsewhere. Dio Cassius, however, put forward an alternative explanation for the outbreak of the revolt: "Claudius had given sums of money to the leading Britons and according to Catus Decianus, the procurator of the island, the money had to be returned together the rest. The confiscation of this money was the pretext for war. In addition, Seneca, with a view to a good rate of interest, had lent the reluctant islanders 40,000,000 sesterces and had then called it all in at once and not very gently. So rebellion broke out."[66] In addition to resentment about the collection of money, Cassius Dio blamed Boudica for the rebellion.

She and the Iceni first struck at Camulodunum. As a Druidic priestess, Boudica performed a divination procedure before her people rode into the city. Hares were considered to be beasts who have a strong bond with the gods, and the Celts were forbidden to hunt them, believing that would bring cowardice to he who hunted it. Before they went into battle, Boudica released a hare, and the animal then ran alongside the Celtic troops, which they interpreted as a sign that the divine spirit was with them. Upon observing this, Boudica cried out, "I thank you, Andraste, and call upon you as woman speaking to woman." Andraste was believed to be the war goddess who was married to their chief god. The rabbit was the animal symbol of Andraste.

---

[64] Tacitus, *The Annals*, 14.31.
[65] *Boudica Britannia; Rebel War Leader and Queen* by Aldhouse-Green (2006). Harlow, Pearson Longman.
[66] Dio Cassius, *Roman History*, 62.2.1-4.

Before entering the city, it was reported that the Roman statue saluting victory fell, as predicted by the female Roman soothsayers, and when the Roman settlers who lived in Camulodunum saw the thunderous collapse of the statue over the Temple of Claudius, they panicked. According to Tacitus, "Women in restless ecstasy rushed among the people, and with frantic screams denounced impending ruin."

Indeed, Boudica's attack was as sudden as it was surprising. The ancient writers claimed that traitorous Trinovantes were living in Camulodunum among the Romans, and that they conspired to make the Iceni assault more successful.

The Celts made their strength known by devastating Camulodunum, which lacked the kind of city walls, garrisons, and fortifications that the Romans typically relied on. Moreover, the Roman military personnel stationed there were veterans of former wars, and many of them were no longer physically capable of confronting the Celts. These older Roman soldiers donned their old armor against the Celtic hordes and hoped for reinforcements, only for Boudica and her forces to slaughter them and destroy the governmental buildings and bathhouses. The Iceni devastated the Temple of Claudius and burned it, and then they set the farming sheds aflame. Recently, archeologists have found evidence of a layer of ash beneath the ruins of the Temple of Claudius, physical proof that the Celts did in fact burn the site.

Boudica then led her troops into the outlying neighborhoods and fields, where the cavalry rode in on their chariots and hacked at the Romans. Then they disembarked and attacked the knife-wielding centurions scattered among the lands of the province. The Celts thrust their spears toward the exposed legs of these Roman defenders, and as they all began to fall, oxen pulled away from their yokes and trampled those who still stood.

Upon hearing of the asault, the Roman procurator Catus Decianus dispatched some of his divisions under Petilius Cerialis to wipe out this insurrection, but Deicanus only sent in about 200 Roman centurions, clearly not enough to counter the Celts. Indeed, when the legions arrived, the predictions of the soothsayers continued to come true. For two whole days, Boudica and her rebels slaughtered the Romans, many of whom fled to woodlands outside of Camulodunum. The timid legion commander, Petilius Cerialis, and his bodyguards escaped and hid out at the village of Lindum while Boudica and her forces continued to massacre the Roman inhabitants of the outlying districts. They also smashed the religious symbols adorning the area.

In the wake of the attack, male prisoners were nailed to crosses or burned alive, and the remaining Roman settlers, including old women and children, were slaughtered. The Celts typically never took prisoners, and this would be no exception. The statues and tombs of Roman soldiers there were also torn apart and destroyed. Archeologists came upon the tombstone of Favonius Facilis, a Roman veteran buried there, and the face on his tombstone had been chopped off by a sharp instrument. The sculpture of Longinus, a mercenary who fought for Rome, was hacked up, and the bronze head of Claudius was chopped off with an axe.

Eventually, Boudica and the Celts razed the entire city of Camulodunum, and in short order, the Romans in the neighboring territories sought aid. They were understandably terrified that Boudica and her rebellious forces would attack their settlements as well, but they would find little help abroad. In fact, when Nero learned the news, he exiled Cerialis and commanded Governor Suetonius to put an end to the uprising. There had been rebellions before, but this one seemed to involve the entire Celtic population and threatened to upend the Romans entirely.

As Boudica massacred the entire population of Camulodunum and razed the settlement to the ground, Suetonius was busily engaged in Mona and could not help. The Ninth Roman Division, led by Rufus, marched to aid the settlement but was routed by the Iceni.

Verulamium (modern St. Albans) was called "Gwerllam" by the tribes at the time, meaning "Dwelling of the Water." Its indigenous tribes were called the Casii or Casavellauni, and their former leader was Caractacus. The ancient writer Tacitus, whose father-in-law Agricola governed this area, noted that the area was distinctively Roman at the time of Boudica's revolt. Emperor Nero granted Verulamium a charter in 58 CE, and it became the Roman headquarters. Verulamium had willingly become a Roman vassal state, so Boudica felt little compassion even for the Celtic people of the town.

Boudica galloped into Verulamium along with her forces, and they set about plundering the Roman population there. The Celts took gold and silver, as well as grain from the warehouses the Romans had built. Frantically, centurions notified Suetonius, who was on the march, that Boudica's forces outnumbered the Romans.

At this time, Suetonius had two legions with him, Legio XIV and Legio XX, but there were not many soldiers in the fortifications and ramparts the Romans had left in Verulamium before the assault. In the wake of the attack, fires raged in every quarter, and Suetonius quickly sent word across Britain's south calling upon the *Legio II Augusta* troops under the command of Posthumus to move north to meet the Iceni. Posthumus never arrived, and by the time the bloody battle was over, Verulamium was left in ruins. As many as 70,000 from both sides died in the fighting.

Dumnonia was a Celtic tribal region that was frequented by the Phoenicians from whom the Celts bought swords and learned how to fashion tin into tools and weapons. The capital city of Dumnonia was called *Isca Dumnonia* by the Celts and was settled when Julius Caesar first entered Britain. The term "Dumnonia" meant "waters of the Dumnonii," and the River Exe ran through this valley. The capital was later called "Exeter," as it is today, and it was reportedly a walled city with large buildings and a substantial fortification. Although it was considered a vassal state for Rome, only the capital was allied with the Romans, and the outlying districts remained fiercely Celtic. Many of the most capable men there had already left to join the rebellion, while the rest gathered up arms to protect their people if the Romans were to come through there during the campaign.

One of the reasons Posthumus never came to help Suetonius in Verulamium was the fact that the Celts in the countryside were loyal to Boudica, and he believed that his forces would be in too much danger marching through Dumnonia. At the end of Boudica's revolt, Posthumus committed suicide rather than face Roman justice for his failure to join the other Roman legions.

Meanwhile, the Iceni generally used guerilla tactics. They split up into smaller groups and hid in the deeply forested areas, conducting surveillance operations on sections of the Romans' main force and picking off those on the edges with spears. That served to disrupt the marching patterns of the Roman legions and disrupted their progress. Once the Celts located a small unit, they brought word back, increased the size of their forces, and raced toward the Roman soldiers headlong. They also ambushed the Romans from behind the rocks and trees of the Midlands.

Whenever such an ambush happened, Romans turned and threw javelins at the Celts, and then they jabbed them with their sharpened lances. However, the Celtic horses were well-trained mounts capable of pivoting in an instant, and Boudica's armies constantly moved, while the Romans marched in compulsive columns and stopped from time to time to encamp. As a result, Suetonius's greatest challenge was to find the Celts and chase them down.

The Romans traced the whereabouts of Boudica and the Celtic forces and soon realized that Londinium was their next target. At that time, Londinium was a collection of wooden dwellings that served as shops for merchants. It was a center of commerce, making it a prime target, and as the Iceni neared Londinium, Suetonius and a small band of his men lurked in the nearby forest.

Suetonius sent on his scouts to locate Boudica and her force, but when they returned, they reported that Boudica and her massive armies numbered about 230,000. Suetonius discovered that there were no city walls around Londinium, and he was painfully aware there were not enough Roman defenders to protect the town.

To help alleviate the danger that faced the Romans there, Suetonius sent messengers to the settlers of the town, offering them safe passage. Many accepted, and lines of Roman men, women, and children abandoned the town, but others remained behind. Those who stayed felt that they would be safe there, but others were too sick or infirm to move. Suetonius then withdrew and moved south of the town.

Boudica and the Iceni rampaged across Londinium, going from house to house and killing the inhabitants. The Iceni plundered the place and smashed the statues of the Roman gods upon the cobblestones in front. Bodies, lumber, and tools were heaped upon the walkways, and the Romans who had remained there were slaughtered without mercy. As Tacitus put it, Suetonius had "decided to sacrifice the one town to save the general situation. Undeflected by the tears and prayers of those who begged for his help he gave the signal to move, taking into his company any who could join it. Those who were unfit for war because of their sex, or too aged to go or too fond of the place to leave were butchered by the enemy."[67]

Having taken Londinium, the rebels quickly moved on to Verulamium, where the massacres continued. "The same massacre continued at Verulamium, for the barbarian British, happiest when looting and unenthusiastic about real effort, bypassed the forts and garrisons and headed for where they knew lay the maximum of undefended booty. Something like 70,000 Roman citizens and other friends of Rome died in the places I have mentioned; the Britons took no prisoners sold no captives as slaves and went in for none of the usual trading of war. They wasted no time in getting down to the bloody business of hanging, burning and crucifying. It was as if they feared that retribution might catch up [to] them while their vengeance was only half complete."[68]

While the Celts were busy destroying Verulamium, Suetonius was scouting out the best possible site for a decisive battle. The Roman legions were astounded that Suetonius did not lead them into the heart of the towns of Verulamium and Londinium, but he was a skilled commander. Boudica's army heavily outnumbered his forces, and it was his responsibility to halt this rebellion before it encompassed the whole region. Realizing that his men might mistake his moves for cowardice, Suetonius halted the Roman army and spoke up about Boudica's forces, which they were carefully surveilling. He told his men, "There, you see more women than warriors. Unwarlike, unarmed, they will give way the moment they have recognized that sword and that courage of their conquerors, which have so often routed them. Even among many legions, it is a few who really decide the battle, and it will enhance their glory that a small force should earn the renown of an entire army."

Ever so carefully the Roman legions marched onward. When Suetonius selected a battlefield, he kept in mind the fact that there were nearly five times as many Celts as there were Romans, so he chose an area that had a narrow open field lined on either side by towering trees. The field was accessible, wide at the top end, and narrower at the far end. He instructed his men to unleash their pilums (spears), and the main body was to stand in close rank, holding up their shields. The shields they carried were large and covered their whole bodies from neck to toe. He further instructed them to get into a straight-on formation. "Give no thought to plunder," he cautioned them, as he knew there would not be any time for that.

For their part, the Celts' confidence in victory was such that they brought their wives and children with them and left them in carts stationed at the edge of the battlefield.[69] Both Suetonius and Boudica are said to have inspired their troops with rousing speeches before Suetonius gave the signal for the battle to commence. The climactic clash of the uprising would be known as the Battle of Watling Street.

Watling Street today is a highway built upon an old Roman road that leads from St. Albans to

---

[67] Tacitus, *The Annals*, 14.33.
[68] Tacitus, *The Annals*, 14.33.
[69] Tacitus, *The Annals*, 14.33.

the city of Wroxeter. Historians believe that the battlefield may have been in the Roman town of Lactodoruii (today's Towcester). Watling Street ran northwest to southeast, ending about 100 miles north of London. It paralleled the River Tove, which the Romans utilized to haul their equipment by oxen. Boudica was east of them with her forces. The Iceni fighting force led the advance, followed by every other available Iceni Celt, including women and children. They had numerous carts loaded with supplies, as if a whole population was migrating en masse. The Romans numbered about 10,000.

Boudica and her army approached and roared out in rage when they saw the Roman legions. The centurions first thrust their javelins at Boudica and her army, but even as the front line of the Iceni was decimated, hordes of others leaped over their bodies and rushed at the enemy. Then Boudica called for a second onslaught. Chariots crashed into each other, throwing one or both of their riders about, and groups of Roman cavalry attacked the Celtic infantry. Arrows flew from the enemies' archers, and many hit their mark, leaving many Celts bleeding out on the ground.

The Romans commenced a charge and pushed up against the lightly clad Celts, thrusting at them with short swords and rotating the front lines constantly to ensure that there were fresh soldiers to carry on the fight. Roman cavalry encountered the wild cavalry of the Celts. Men who were unhorsed dragged those still mounted to the ground and fought them with swords.

At one point, Suetonius tried to divide his forces into three divisions, but the battlefield became crowded and chaotic. The killing continued until nightfall, and as the Celts fell back, the Romans began plundering the field. Boudica then dispatched her warriors to move forward yet again and push back the Romans, but Suetonius wisely had his army create wedge-like formations in "V" patterns, which left the Iceni trapped between the crush of Roman legionnaires.

As Celtic soldiers turned to retreat, they ran into wagons of supplies with women driving them forth, and confusion broke out. The Romans had no mercy for any Celt in their vicinity, and by the end, the ground was littered with dead Celts. Tacitus wrote that "the remaining Britons fled with difficulty since their ring of wagons blocked the outlets. The Romans did not spare even the women. Baggage animals too, transfixed with weapons added to the heaps of dead."[70]

Boudica survived the battle, but it is said she retreated to the woods and poisoned herself. That act was immortalized in Glover's tragedy:

> "Tell them, I go out fortune to restore,
>
> If unsuccessful, never to return,
>
> Should that stern doom attend me, bid them take

---

[70] Tacitus, *The Annals*, 14.33.

> The last, best gift, which dying I can leave them;
>
> That of my blood no part may prove dishonors."

Although it is a myth, it is said that she was buried with great honor and that her remains are buried deep below Platform 10 at Kings Cross Station in Greater London, but the location of the Battle of Watling Street is still unknown today. Theories range from King's Cross in London to Church Stowe in Northampton.

The Aftermath of the Uprising

Boudica's defeat was followed by a program of severe suppression of the indigenous population, initiated by Suetonius. Indeed, the measures he introduced to pacify Britain were so severe that he was eventually recalled to Rome and replaced by Publius Petronius Turpilianus, who tried a gentler approach to pacification. Neither approach proved entirely successful, and sporadic revolts continued to break out until Agricola put a definitive end to any hope the Britons had of expelling their conquerors.

A statue of Agricola

Not all of the British tribes had taken part in the revolt, but according to Tacitus, whether they were hostile or neutral, they all suffered from the effects of the conflict. One of the major disasters stemming from the revolt was famine caused by the failure to sow crops. The situation created difficulties between the tribes who all jostled to secure food and security for their people. In due course, the basic problems of supply were resolved, but the underlying dissatisfaction remained, and internal wars became endemic. Tacitus records further revolts against the Romans by Cartimandua and Venutius in 69 CE. He described Venutius as a "man of barbarous spirit who hated the Roman power."[71] He also had a grievance against his former wife, Cartimandua, who had thrown him out and taken his armor bearer, Vellocatus, as her husband. The Brigantes were shocked by their queen's actions and declared for her former husband. In desperation, she turned to the Romans—against whom she had so recently fought—to restore her to her throne.

While the Romans secured the queen's safety, as Tacitus had put it, "they were left with a war to fight."[72] In 70 CE, Quintus Petillius Cerialis took a Roman force from Lincoln to York to defeat Venutius near Stanwick, resulting in the Brigantes and Parisii tribes being further assimilated into the empire and increasing the Romanization of the population. Frontinus succeeded Cerialis as governor in 74 CE and subdued the Silures and a number of smaller tribes in Wales, establishing a new base at Caerleon. To secure the area, he also built a series of smaller forts, approximately 10 miles apart, where auxiliary units were stationed. It is likely he built the fort at Pumsaint in the west of Wales to guard the gold mines at Dolaucothi. He retired in 78 CE and was replaced as governor by Gnaeus Julius Agricola, Tacitus's father-in-law, which ensured that his deeds were well known throughout the Roman world.

In 64 CE, Agricola was appointed quaestor in Asia under Proconsul Lucius Salvius Otho Titianus. During this period, his daughter, Julia Agricola, was born, but his son died in the same year. He became a tribune of the plebs in 66 CE and praetor in 68 CE, working for Galba. When Nero committed suicide, the Year of the Four Emperors found Agricola's family involved in the conflicts. Agricola's mother was murdered by Otho's troops in 69 CE, and Agricola sided with Vespasian. When Vespasian succeeded in becoming emperor, Agricola was given command of the Legio XX Valeria Victrix, stationed in Britain.

At this point, Bolanus was the governor of Britain, and when Agricola arrived to take up his new post, he found that there was considerable unrest once again on the island. Agricola's first task was to re-impose discipline within his own legion, which had grown lax under his predecessor. He then set about helping to consolidate Roman rule. In 71 CE, Bolanus was replaced as governor by Quintus Petillius Cerialis, and it was under him that Agricola was able to display his talents in the campaign against the Brigantes. In 73 CE, Agricola's command came to an end, and he was appointed to govern Gallia Aquitania, where he remained until 77 CE before being recalled to Rome. Once there, he was appointed suffect consul, and he betrothed his daughter to Tacitus, with the wedding scheduled to take place the following year. It was quite the year for Agricola, for he was also appointed to the College of Pontiffs and became the new governor of Britain.

Once more, Agricola arrived find Britain riven with unrest. He employed a two-pronged policy to pacify the island: short-term military action and longer-term programs of assimilation. Initially, he had to deal with the Ordovices in Northern Wales, as they had wiped out the Roman

---

[71] Tacitus, *Histories*, 3.45.
[72] Tacitus, *Histories*, 3.45.

garrison there. He marched north and routed them in a short, bloody campaign. He then headed to Mona to complete the campaign that had been started by Suetonius and interrupted by Boudicca's revolt. There, he forced the local population to surrender.

In conjunction with this and other campaigns, Agricola sought to accelerate the process of Romanizing the native aristocracy, which had proven unsuccessful in the past. From the bungled attempt, he learned to involve the locals in the Imperial cult at Colchester, adopting a more systematic and extended policy. "The following winter was taken up with the soundest projects. In order to encourage rough men who lived in scattered settlements, and were thus only too ready to fall to fighting, to live in a peaceful and inactive manner by offering them the consequent pleasures of life, Agricola urged them privately and helped the officials to build temples, public squares with public buildings and houses. He praised those who responded quickly and severely criticized the laggards. In this way competition for public recognition took the place of compulsion."[73]

Agricola realized the long-term future of Roman rule depended on the younger generation of Britons being won over to the Roman way of life. To this end, he ensured that the children of all the leading figures in British society were given a Roman education that promoted the arts. The Latin language was taught, and the result, according to Tacitus, was that those who had once shunned the language now sought fluency and elegance in it.[74] Roman dress was encouraged, and the wearing of the toga became commonplace. Romans introduced British aristocracy to the delights of assembly rooms, bathing, and smart dinner parties. In one of his more cynical moments, Tacitus noted, "In their inexperience the Britons called it civilization when it was really all part of their servitude."[75]

Agricola, however, found there was still work to be done on the military side. In 79 CE, he moved against the Brigantes in the north and the Selgova in the south of Scotland, and by dint of overwhelming military superiority, he forced them into submission.

Cerialis's earlier campaigns against the Brigantes had brought Scotland to the attention of the Romans, and archaeological evidence suggests that following their success against the Brigantes, the Romans penetrated Scotland and built military camps as far north as the Gask Ridge, controlling the glens and providing access to and from the Scottish Highlands and Lowlands. In his account of Agricola's campaign in Scotland, Tacitus does not state that the Romans had returned to lands they had previously occupied, but it is almost certain this was the case. Whether these early attempts at settlement were overrun by the northern tribes or simply abandoned is unclear.

From Tacitus, it is known that Agricola advanced into Scotland. In 80 CE, he reached the River

---

[73] Tacitus, *The Life of Cnæus Julius Agricola*, 21.
[74] Tacitus, *The Life of Cnæus Julius Agricola*, 21.
[75] Tacitus, *The Life of Cnæus Julius Agricola*, 21.

Tay and remained in Scotland until 81 CE. During this period, he quashed what was relatively ineffective opposition and established forts throughout the south of Scotland.[76] He returned to Scotland after a brief visit to the south in 82 CE, and he sailed to Kintyre in Argyllshire, moving slowly northward along Scotland's eastern and northern coasts in the following two years. In this campaign, he used a coordinated strategy, employing both land and naval forces, and it was during this period that he also sent ships to investigate the island of Ireland.[77] He gave sanctuary to an exiled Irish king, and according to Tacitus, he considered invading Ireland by sending a small force to reconnoiter. No trace of it has ever been found, and no invasion materialized.

Agricola's attention then refocused on the campaign at hand, during which the only major confrontation with the indigenous population took place at the Battle of Mons Graupius, where the northern British tribes united briefly under Calgacus to try to defeat the invaders. The exact location of this battle and the date are unknown, but it was most likely fought in 84 CE. The possible locations range from Perthshire to north of the River Dee, Grampian Mount, Kempstone Hill, Megray Hill, or a spot near the Roman camp at Raedykes. The sites in Aberdeenshire are most similar to the site described by Tacitus, but to date, no archaeological evidence for the battle has been found anywhere in Scotland.[78]

At the battle, the Romans were heavily outnumbered by the tribesmen. Normally, British tribes like the Caledonii avoided pitched battles, but on this occasion, for whatever reason, they decided to test themselves directly against the Romans, presumably in an attempt to stop the Roman pillaging of their lands. Tacitus says the Roman force was made up of approximately 17,000 men, 11,000 of whom were auxiliaries recruited from British tribes and other parts of the empire. The number of legionnaires is not known, but there were 3,000 cavalry, suggesting their numbers were not great.[79] Tacitus estimated the Caledonian forces at 30,000.

The tribesmen stationed themselves on higher ground, with some troops placed at the foot of the rise. The whole force was arranged in horseshoe-formation around the hill. On the plain between the opposing armies, the Caledonian chariots raced along both front lines. As was normal in battles at the time, the battle opened with both sides firing missiles at each other, followed by a frontal attack by the Romans on the native lines. The assault force was made up of Batavian and Tungrian swordsmen, who quickly cut the front ranks of their opponents down, trampling on their comrades as they tried to retreat. Agricola initiated an outflanking ploy against those at the top of the hill. It is said the Legionnaires took no part in the battle, during which, according to Tacitus, 10,000 tribesmen were killed at the cost of only 360 auxiliaries. In the end, Tacitus declared that "Britain was completely conquered."[80]

---

[76] Tacitus, *The Life of Cnæus Julius Agricola*, 19-23.
[77] Tacitus, *The Life of Cnæus Julius Agricola*, 24.
[78] Tacitus, *The Life of Cnæus Julius Agricola*, 21-22.
[79] *Mons Graupius AD 83* by D.B. Campbell (2010). Oxford.
[80] Tacitus, *The Life of Cnæus Julius Agricola*, 21-22.

Before he left Scotland, Agricola initiated an extensive program of military road building and the construction of further forts with which to secure his conquests. The lines of military communications of supply with the south were particularly well-fortified. In southeastern Caledonia, in what is now Dumfriesshire and the Kirkcudbright area, further forts were built, securing Roman control over the area.

Agricola was recalled to Rome by Domitian in 84 CE and was replaced in Britain by a series of governors who decided not to build upon his success in Scotland. The fortress at Inchtuthil was dismantled before it was completed, and fortifications at Gask Ridge in Perthshire were abandoned within a few years of Agricola's recall. It seems likely the economic costs involved in any attempt to consolidate Roman rule in Scotland were vastly greater than any return the Romans might expect from controlling the area. Consequently, Roman occupation was withdrawn to a line which, in due course, was established as one of the *limites* of the empire. The concept of the *limites* was that of "defensible" frontiers. In the case of Britain, that frontier became Hadrian's Wall.

By the time Agricola left Britain, it was an imperial province with a substantial military garrison comprising three legions: the II Augusta (stationed at Caerleon), the XX Valeria Victrix (stationed at Deva, now Chester), and the VI Victrix at Eburacum (stationed at what is now York). In addition, there were probably as many as 75 auxiliary units based predominantly in Wales and the north. Despite the wealth these garrisons brought to the areas in which they were based, they remained less Romanized than in the southern part of the island.

Local government was modeled on the cantonal system the Romans had developed in Gaul. There were, by the end of the 1st century CE, 16 distinct civitates, or civic communities. These were the Brigantes, with a capital at Aldborough; the Parisii, whose capital was Brough on Humber; the Silures, based in Caerwent; the Iceni at Caistor by Norwich; the Cantiaci at Canterbury; the Carvetii Durotiges at Dorchester; Dorset; the Dumnoni at Exeter; the Corieltauvi at Leicester; the Catuvellauni at Verulamium; the Atrbates at Silchester; the Belgae at Winchester; and the Cornovii at Wroxeter. In addition to these, there were three separate Roman coloniae at Colchester, Lincoln, and Glevum, now Gloucester. A fourth was added in the 3rd century CE at York. Londinium, the provincial capital, had an indeterminate status. The civitates were necessarily large and were further subdivided into as many as 70 lesser urban centers that served the countryside away from the main towns. None of the towns were particularly well-endowed with public buildings, though they were quite large for the time. In the 1st century CE, there were no defences for the towns, though these were added in later years (why is unclear). The whole province was ruled from Londinium until the 3rd century CE, when rule was divided between Londinium and York.

This essentially federal structure was run by a combination of different groups. There was no civil service—as the term would be understood today—in the empire at this time. The most senior office holders served periods of varying lengths as administrators in the provinces at specific periods in their careers. They progressed through a series of posts designed to give them military and administrative experience so that anyone reaching the highest levels of government had experience in all levels of the work undertaken in governing the empire. More minor officials were often seconded from the army. The emperor was the head of the whole system, and in him resided the power of imperator and commander-in-chief, though in theory, all of his power was granted at the discretion of the Senate. In practice, it was his control of the army that was the basis of his power.

Provinces like Britain that had substantial military garrisons were kept under the direct control of the emperor. In Britain, any governors appointed were the personal choices of the emperor and were invariably men that he thought he could trust. Governors in Britain were also expected to add to the appointing emperor's prestige through military success. The earliest governors of Britain were drawn from ex-consuls usually at the apex of their political careers who had proven to be skilled administrators. Consequently, in the early days of the Roman conquest, power was given to the emperor's personal representative rather than to institutions. As Roman rule was consolidated in the 1st century CE, the scale of bureaucracy increased, and the subdivision of Britain is a classic example of how the role of the governor had been reduced and that of administrators had increased.

Before the conquest, the countryside was farmed extensively, and this remained the province's mainstay. Estimates suggest that 90% of the population lived on the land and continued to inhabit traditional farmsteads. About 1% of sites became villas, some of which were built almost immediately after the invasion of 43 CE and continued throughout the period of occupation. Though they were small compared to those of the Mediterranean region, the existence of refined mosaics is evidence of the emergence of a wealthy and sophisticated native aristocracy embracing Roman culture. Britain's mineral deposits—especially gold, silver, and lead—continued to be exploited, and local craft-based production was encouraged by the Romans.

While Britain expanded its mining activities, food production, and manufactured goods, it did not really become a major supplier of anything vital to the empire. It did, however, become even wealthier than it had been before the invasion, and the population enjoyed greatly increased standards of living. Moreover, the land was subjected to the normal asset stripping that came with a Roman conquest, especially in the earliest days following the invasion, when valuables were removed by the army and traders tried to cash in. There is no way of estimating the quantity of bullion taken from Britain as booty, but given the proliferation of gold and silver coinage and the presence of gold artefacts in Iron Age Britain, it must have been considerable.

The gold found in 1990 in Snettisham in Norfolk, for example, was enough to have paid a unit of Roman auxiliaries for an entire year, and that was from a minor, British site that dated back to before the Roman invasion. Metal resources were quickly exploited, and the Romans were mining lead and silver in the Mendips from 49 CE onward. Further mines were in operation soon after in Derbyshire, Yorkshire, and Wales. Gold mining was centered at Dolaucothi in South Wales, and by 75 CE, the Romans were producing significant amounts of the precious metal. Copper, too, was mined from the earliest years after the invasion, though strangely, given the association of Britain with tin, there is little evidence of Roman exploitation of that metal. Iron was mined throughout the island, and the Romans simply took over existing workings, particularly in Sussex. The iron mined there was primarily used by the Roman fleet based at Boulogne.

The wealth taken by traders is a little easier to assess. Raw materials had been a lure for traders for many years, and the opportunity to expand this trade and those presented by access to native tribes as potential markets for goods was seized upon by many traders and merchants. The money brought into the country by the troops was certainly a factor in increasing trade. By the time of Agricola's departure, a full 10% of the Roman army was stationed in Britain, and the combined spending power of those troops was a major injection into the British economy. Initially, such an influx of cash would have destabilized the local economies which had been under the control of local chiefs, operating on a small scale. The deficit in goods at a time when buyers were available would have caused inflation and resulted in traders diverting goods to Britain to take advantage of the profits to be gained there. This unique set of circumstances is thought to explain the very rapid development of Londinium. As early as 50 CE, the city had become the main center for overseas traders.

Roman goods spread rapidly and Samian wares, for example, can be found on a vast majority of indigenous sites from as early as 70 CE. Whether the native products were eclipsed or whether they continued to be produced and sold in some kind of native parallel economy is not clear. After the conquest, Roman coinage spread throughout the island, though slowly at first. Shortages of coins and vast fluctuations in supply suggest that administrative decisions rather than economic necessity governed the supply of money. Initially, the Celtic system of barter and indebtedness seems to have been maintained for a considerable time as Roman coinage gradually became the foremost medium of exchange and trade.

After the conquest, art and culture developed as a hybrid of Celtic and classical Roman features. Various religions, so numerous in the Mediterranean world, spread to Britain in the wake of the polyglot army and its many administrators. Celtic gods continued to be worshipped, but they took on new forms, and the use of Romano-Celtic styles of temples and architecture increased, as did the adoption of Latin epigraphy on altars and dedications. The whole process of amalgamation was speeded up by the habit of Roman soldiers identifying local Celtic gods with members of the Roman pantheon. In this way, specific gods became associated with specific regions and civitates.

This coalescence of Celtic and Roman practice is exemplified by changes in British burial practices. Before the invasion, it was customary for the dead to be buried with animals, and often in wet places. This continued under the Romans, but Roman weapons and sculpture gradually began to be buried along with traditional grave goods. One of the more subtle—some might say insidious—ways in which the Romans altered native practice was in the promotion of the use of small religious objects. These are found widely in both military and civil sites of the period. The small clay figures of the gods are representative of deities such as Venus, but they were produced in such a way as to suggest the traditional mother goddess. A further Romanization of a very British tradition related to human heads. Prior to the invasion, the collecting of human heads and their display was common throughout the island. This practice evolved under the Romans into the use of sculptured stone heads and even bronze ones, many of which have been discovered in British rivers.

In art, new materials, mainly stone sculpture and mosaic, supplanted the Iron Age metalwork of the pre-invasion period. While the mosaics were not always the most exquisite, they did exhibit a specific innovatory blend of Celtic and Roman themes. These developments accelerated a process that had begun early on in the conquest, that of the change from a tribal society to one integrated into the empire. The process was slow, but the spread of everyday items that exhibited Romano-British styles—as opposed to the localized designs that had been the hallmark of pre-invasion native society—certainly helped to reinforce the concept of one people under Rome.

Following the initial period of rapid importation of goods from the rest of the empire, Britain's economy gradually settled down, and industries established in the wake of the conquest thrived, taking an increasingly large share of the market. Roman pottery was replaced by high-quality local products, but in contrast to the situation before the Romans came, the products were now sold and distributed throughout the island rather than made available only in the immediate vicinity of their production.

With this new trade came improvements in communications systems. The improvements were both the result and the cause of increased trade and led to the positioning of centers of trade on navigable rivers to reduce costs. Roman military roads were always well-built, but the exploitation of Britain's rivers cut haulage costs in half, further stimulating trade. All in all, the early years of the Roman occupation proved beneficial to the local Britons and the Empire as well.

The period of the Roman invasions of Britain and the initial conquest of the island was a traumatic one in British history. For the first time, the greater part of the island became part of a world ruled by an alien, Mediterranean culture. It was a time when the outside world stimulated extensive change, though native characteristics continued to play a prominent part in molding society. The lives of many people changed, but it is clear that some people's lives changed far more than others. Many of the changes were the direct result of the Roman occupation while others evolved to meet the new economic and social situation resulting from the conquest.

Society gradually became less and less dominated by tribal divisions, and this coincided with the development of the concept of Britannia as a single place.

This breakdown in the regional system, which was so solidly entrenched in pre-invasion British society, was accompanied by increasing social and economic differentiation as wealth and power became more and more concentrated in the hands of those who most enthusiastically embraced Roman culture and values. This elite became an integral part of a culture that networked with their social and economic equals in other parts of the Roman Empire. Ordinary members of the population became increasingly dependent on this new class. The military installations the Romans installed as part of their pursuit of pacification removed all political power from the natives. As the army settled in Britain, they inevitably became somewhat naturalized, reflecting a mixture of Roman and native characteristics, while remaining highly Romanized. Beyond the frontiers following Agricola's campaign, these tribes remained, for the most part, unaffected by Rome, except when Rome decided to undertake one of its periodic assaults on their territory. Gradually, even these areas fell under Roman influence, if not direct control, and contact with the Romans led to changes within their societies.

In 55 BCE, Britain was a relatively prosperous and populated land and should have been able to ward off the initial attacks of the Romans relatively easily, if only they had unified under a single leader. The reality, however, was that the regionally-based tribes were far too independently minded, the regional economies far too insular, and attitudes and loyalties far too parochial for them to ever seriously consider banding together for a common cause, even if that cause was their own survival. Their whole way of life was based on local groups looking after specific interests, taking advantage of any weakness in their neighbors. It was in this context that the Romans found they could exploit local rivalries, first supporting one local king against another, then changing sides to enable them to gain control over a population that, if they had had to rely on military might alone, would have proven impossible.

Military might, however, was a crucial factor in the Roman success. As in other conquests, the discipline of the Legions, the tactics employed, and the military genius exhibited by some of its commanders meant the Roman army was more than a match for any contemporary foe. Only a unified British defiance would have had any chance of repelling Roman invasions, but that was never a realistic possibility.

As such, the resistance would be left for a leader like Boudicca, who nearly 2,000 years later is still held out as a symbol of liberty. Hers is a story of the tremendous response that oppressed people sometimes exert in the face of impossible odds. She is also a model for womanhood, as she never let her gender interfere with ambition. The story ensures that while Boudica may have lived and died in the 1st century, her legacy has lasted well into the 21st century.

Paul Walter's picture of a statue commemorating Boudica at Westminster

Further Reading

Aldhouse-Green, M. (2006). Boudica Britannia: Rebel, War-Leader and Queen. Pearson Longman.

de la Bédoyère, Guy (2003). "Bleeding from the Roman Rods: Boudica". Defying Rome: The Rebels of Roman Britain. Tempus: Stroud.

Böckl, Manfred (2005). Die letzte Königin der Kelten [The last Queen of the Celts] (in German). Berlin: Aufbau Verlag.

Cassius Dio Cocceianus (1914–1927). Dio's Roman History. 8. Earnest Cary trans. Cambridge, Massachusetts: Harvard University Press.

Collingridge, Vanessa (2004). Boudica. London: Ebury.

Dudley, Donald R; Webster, Graham (1962). The Rebellion of Boudicca. London: Routledge.

Fraser, Antonia (1988). The Warrior Queens. London: Weidenfeld and Nicolson.

Godsell, Andrew (2008). "Boadicea: A Woman's Resolve". Legends of British History. Wessex Publishing.

Hingley, Richard; Unwin, Christina (2004). Boudica: Iron Age Warrior Queen. London: Hambledon and London.

Roesch, Joseph E. (2006). Boudica, Queen of The Iceni. London: Robert Hale Ltd.

Tacitus, Cornelius (1948). Tacitus on Britain and Germany. H. Mattingly trans. London: Penguin.

Tacitus, Cornelius (1989). The Annals of Imperial Rome. M. Grant trans. London: Penguin.

Taylor, John (1998). Tacitus and the Boudican Revolt. Dublin: Camvlos.

Webster, Graham (1978). Boudica. Totowa, NJ: Rowman and Littlefield.

Cottrell, Leonard (1958). The Great Invasion. Evans Brothers Limited.

Printed in Great Britain
by Amazon